Funny Thing About Minnesota...

Funny Thing About Minnesota...

THE RISE, FALL, AND REBIRTH OF THE TWIN CITIES COMEDY SCENE

Patrick Strait

MINNESOTA HISTORICAL SOCIETY PRESS

mnhspress.org

The Minnesota Historical Society Press is a member of the Association of University Presses.

Manufactured in the United States

10 9 8 7 6 5 4 3 2 1

♾ The paper used in this publication meets the minimum requirements of the American National Standard for Information Sciences—Permanence for Printed Library Materials, ANSI Z39.48–1984.

International Standard Book Number
ISBN: 978-1-68134-186-6 (paper)
ISBN: 978-1-68134-187-3 (e-book)

Library of Congress Control Number: 2020947708
This and other MNHS Press books are available from popular e-book vendors.

Contents

1

A Bar Called Mickey Finn's

Downtown Minneapolis in the late 1970s wasn't lacking for entertainment. Disco was alive and booming at Scotties on Seventh. Scotties catered to a relatively posh crowd of revelers who were ready to pay a cover charge, adhere to a dress code, and shell out for more expensive drinks. Around the corner, on Hennepin Avenue's notorious Block E, Moby Dick's bar was packed with younger drinkers looking to party, whether in the form of fighting, flirting, sex, or drugs. Over at First Avenue and Seventh Street, the popular Uncle Sam's was part of a nationwide franchise of dance clubs. The venue had not yet become its more famous successor, First Avenue, and was still years away from its *Purple Rain* fame, but at the time, Uncle Sam's was known for its progressive dance nights and party atmosphere.

But while there was plenty to do in Minneapolis, there wasn't anything unique driving people into the city. Bar owners competed to find new ways to attract attention and customers. Steve Billings was one of those bar owners.

At the time, Billings was the proud owner of two bars in the Twin Cities. In St. Paul, he had Denny's Loft, a popular bar known for dancing and live country music. This was Billings's moneymaker, as it attracted a younger crowd that was interested in dressing up, having drinks, and letting loose. Then there was Mickey Finn's in Minneapolis.

Located just outside of the downtown core in St. Anthony, Mickey Finn's was housed in the first floor of the Minneapolis Labor Union building at 312 Central Avenue Southeast. The bar's business model was simple: each day pipe fitters, boilermakers, and other laborers would manage union business upstairs and then stop downstairs at Mickey Finn's to drink in the evening.

"The building housed the offices for most of the unions in Minneapolis," says Billings. "It was busier than Hades Monday through Thursday, because we'd get the lunch crowd from those offices, and then the unions would have meetings at night before heading down to the bar. Problem was, there were no meetings on Friday or Saturday nights."

In 1977, Billings wasn't trying to make comedy history. He wasn't planning to provide the kindling that would spark a comedy revolution or build a stage that would elevate some legendary comedic voices. He was just trying to make a few bucks on an off night at the bar.

At that time, most people in the country experienced stand-up comedy only through their televisions, such as the occasional set by Bob Newhart or George Carlin on late-night talk shows. There were only a few places in the country you could go to see live stand-up on a regular basis: New York, where the original Improv comedy club opened in the early sixties and was followed by Catch a Rising Star and a few others; or Los Angeles, where the second Improv franchise location opened in the mid-seventies. One weekend in 1977, one of Billings's bartenders took a trip to California, and while there he wandered into the LA Improv one night to check it out. When he returned to Minnesota, he raved about it to Billings, sharing details about the crowds, the comics, the show, and everything that made it a revolutionary entertainment experience.

The idea of an entire live show focused on stand-up comedy was unheard of, especially in Minnesota. Still, the seed was planted. "I had never been to a stand-up comedy show in my life," Billings remembers. "I'd probably seen a comedian on Johnny Carson or something, but never a full show. But I figured nobody else in the city was doing it, so we might as well give it a shot."

With no experience and no comedy playbook to follow, Billings devised a plan to invite anyone and everyone with aspirations of making people laugh to get onstage. It would be something of a free-for-all event that would, he hoped, put butts in the seats and sell a few more beers.

In late 1977, Billings launched a ten-week comedy competition at Mickey Finn's called "The First-Annual Minneapolis Stand-Up Comedy Competition."

"We advertised in all the Minneapolis newspapers, and we got a pretty good number of people who came out and did their routine," Billings says. "We'd let anyone who wanted to try get onstage."

Because stand-up comedy in the Twin Cities was essentially nonexistent, the talent pool for the ten-week showcase was, to put it mildly, shallow. "We had a guy who went by the name of Chazy Bland," Billings recalls with a laugh. "I don't remember what his real name was, but he was not real funny. But he kept coming back to the bar every week, so we just kept letting him be in the competition, and he'd bomb every week."

"You know, you'd get some who were funny and some who weren't, but we had to have people in the show to make it work."

Even though the laughs were few and far between, Billings was committed to the idea. With no real overhead in terms of production costs or having to pay the talent, there seemed little reason to give up on the series, despite its slow start. Still, the bar struggled to find an audience those first few months, with only ten or twelve people in the crowd on a good night. And then, Billings caught a break.

"One day I got a call from a columnist from the *Minneapolis Tribune* who saw our ad," Billings says. "They were always looking for something to write about and had never heard anything about stand-up comedy, so I invited him down to the show that night. He thought it was pretty good, so he plugged it in his column, and the next week we had a lot more people coming in to check it out."

The audiences slowly began to build. It still wasn't a home run by any means, but the novelty of live comedy was enough to set Mickey Finn's apart in the crowded world of Minneapolis entertainment.

At the end of the ten weeks, Mickey Finn's crowned its first comedy champion: a man named Gary Johnson. Though it may not be a name you'll hear when learning about the comedy pioneers of the era,

Johnson's is arguably the first name on the list of notable stand-up comedians in Twin Cities history.

"[Minneapolis television station] KSTP had him [Johnson] and me on a TV show one night, and that got us a little bit of excitement," Billings recalls. While the show may have been a modest launching pad for Johnson, the real achievement was the interest it built locally around the idea of stand-up comedy.

At the time, Billings had a regular Saturday-night performer known as "Arnie Chuckle: The One-Man Band." One night, Arnie couldn't make his regular gig, so Billings decided to host a comedy night, outside of the competition series. It drew about the same number of people to the bar as a typical Arnie Chuckle show—and that, along with the fact that Billings didn't have to pay the performers, spelled the end for Arnie Chuckle and the beginning of weekly Saturday-night comedy shows at Mickey Finn's.

"We didn't have a full house every night, but we had a pretty good-sized crowd," says Billings. "The bar wasn't all that big to begin with, maybe fifty or sixty people [capacity], so even if we had thirty or forty it would be pretty full. My philosophy was that I'd rather be open and break even than be closed and broke, so it made sense." He adds that, although the comedy nights brought in enough money to pay the bartender and keep the lights on, "it certainly wasn't a big moneymaker, by any means. But that was fine, because I was thinking it would get our name out there for the lunch crowd."

Billings was satisfied with the turnout and the name recognition the new comedy attraction was bringing to Mickey Finn's, but his Minneapolis bar still was not nearly as lucrative as his other establishment. Not only was Denny's Loft attracting bigger crowds, but the patrons were there to spend money. "The problem early on with the comedy crowd was that they'd come in, order one drink, and then sip on it all night," Billings says.

With his attention and time divided between the two bars, it was becoming too much for Billings. "I was bouncing between Denny's Loft and Mickey Finn's, wearing myself out, and it just didn't make any sense."

The solution was simple: he needed to find someone who was

passionate and trustworthy enough to handle the responsibilities for running the comedy shows, leaving Billings and his staff to manage the regular bar operations. He found Jeff Gerbino.

Gerbino, an Irish-Italian New Yorker, had participated in the comedy contest at Mickey Finn's, reaching the finals before losing to Johnson. "He had a very scripted act," Gerbino snaps when the name Gary Johnson is mentioned. The contest took place more than forty years ago, but you can still hear a hint of annoyance in his voice over losing. "But sometimes coming in second teaches you something," he adds. "Plus, I ended up in a hell of a lot better position than he did."

Gerbino expressed immediate interest in being involved with Mickey Finn's comedy night, and that was all the convincing the bar owner needed. "I decided I'd pay Jeff Gerbino a few pennies just to coordinate things, get the acts lined up and stuff like that," says Billings.

With Gerbino at the helm, Mickey Finn's began to develop and grow its reputation as a comedy room. Gerbino went about arranging the talent and hitting the streets to drum up business. "For the first maybe six to nine months," he recalls, "I knew that we needed to find a way to get people in the doors and fill a two-hour show."

In addition to keeping the bar's owner happy, Gerbino was also determined to keep the shows going in order to sustain his own opportunities to perform. "I wanted to do comedy, plain and simple," he says. "At that point, there was nowhere else you could get up and do jokes like that. I had to keep the place running if I wanted somewhere to do it."

Along the way, Gerbino met Scott Hansen and Bill Bauer. Both were regulars of the comedy nights, with Bauer dabbling in the performance aspect before encouraging Hansen to try it as well. As both proved themselves worthy of the stage time, the two aspiring comics soon became partners with Gerbino in helping to build the room—in some cases, literally.

One day, the trio decided the bar needed a stage to create a more official-looking performance space. With limited resources available, they stacked plywood on top of milk crates to form a stage. Meanwhile, Gerbino learned that an Italian restaurant in town was closing,

Jeff Gerbino at Mickey Finn's. (Courtesy of Jeff Gerbino)

and he convinced the owner to give him the portraits of comedians like Bill Cosby and Richard Pryor that were hanging on the walls, which he used to bring some comedy-focused decor into Mickey Finn's. Gerbino also continued to lead the charge on media outreach and promotion, regularly calling up the local newspapers and radio stations to rave about the hottest ticket in town, taking place at the old union bar.

Gerbino, Hansen, and Bauer did it all while trying to find their own ways as comedians. "There were nights that it would just be me, Bill, and Scott each doing thirty minutes, trying to figure out how to fill the time," Gerbino says.

But the trio soldiered on and gradually built a buzz around the bar that drew in more curious comedy fans, as well as more wannabe comics. "We started getting a lot of people who wanted to get on-stage," Hansen says. "We'd get a lot of the cast of Dudley Riggs who would want to come over and try things, either because they wanted to try stand-up or they wanted to try out some skits that weren't approved by Dudley."

At the time, Dudley Riggs and his Brave New Workshop improv theater essentially had the market cornered for live comedy in Minneapolis. The relatively polished, glitzy performance product of Brave New Workshop was a far cry from the gritty, raw aesthetic of Mickey Finn's, and any comedy connoisseur would have laughed you out of the room, and not in a good way, if you tried to compare the dingy bar to Dudley Riggs's grand presentations. But Mickey Finn's offered a freewheeling, experimental opportunity for comedians that was distinct from the Dudley Riggs approach.

By October of 1978, Mickey Finn's had found its niche. The comedy shows were routinely drawing standing room–only crowds, with customers arriving as much as an hour and a half before showtime to make sure they could snag a table. The rest of the patrons would crowd around the bar and squeeze in among the pinball machines until there was nowhere left to move.

The talent pool began to grow as well, and at times as many as thirty or forty aspiring comedians would be bending Gerbino's, Hansen's, and Bauer's ears to get stage time. Clearly, there was a demand for more shows at the bar.

Alex Cole is frequently credited by other performers as the first stand-up comedian from Minnesota. Even before Mickey Finn's, Cole had built a career doing comedy shows at colleges around the country. Still, he was intrigued by what was going on at this dank

Minneapolis bar and decided to check it out for himself. Before too long, he was one of the onstage regulars.

Cole says that the transformation of Mickey Finn's from ragtag comedy bunker to must-see comedy haven happened quickly. "The first time I went to this place, I was looking around and thinking what a dump it was," Cole recalls with a laugh. "There were maybe six people there, and you had these three young guys doing their best to keep their interest on this little stage they built. Next thing I know, I leave town and come back maybe six months later and there are lines around the block. They really started to find their rhythm."

As the small but mighty comedy club was bringing in more customers and providing valuable stage time to up-and-coming comics, not everyone was happy to see the change in the bar's focus and clientele. "The union guys did not want us there," Gerbino says. "They're trying to drink, and having these young guys with a microphone telling jokes wasn't what they wanted to see. It was a real trial by fire."

"We'd be trying to do the show, and you'd still have the ironworkers at the bar being so loud that you couldn't hear anything," Hansen recalls. "Bill was a Vietnam vet and had a temper, so he decided he was going to handle all this his way. There was one guy in particular, a big, burly pipe fitter named Arnie, and these two used to get on each other constantly. He'd get loud, and Bill would come over and start shouting at him, and Arnie would threaten to throw Bill through the front window of the bar."

To deal with this division between the union boys and the comedy crew, Hansen, Gerbino, and Bauer decided to create a literal divide. "We built a wood partition between the bar and the comedy stage with four-foot-by-eight-foot wood panels," Hansen says. "Then we built a little door for people to go in and out. But it didn't matter. Arnie and Bill would still be at each other all the time. You'd open the door and hear Bill screaming at him, 'Fuck you! Pipe fitters can't hold my ass!' and then the door would close again. But in a way, it brought all of us comedians together. Arnie was the common enemy we needed."

Comedian Paul Dillery didn't take the stage himself until a few years into Mickey Finn's life as a comedy club, but he remembers going there as a fan in those early days and feeling somewhat un-comfortable with the atmosphere. "I remember it was dark and loud. People were drinking and the guys onstage were just trying to keep people's attention," Dillery recalls. "The first time I went it was Scott Hansen, Roman Dicaire, Alex Cole, and Dan Bradley. And I remember thinking that the place felt sort of rough."

Not long after, Dillery would become a regular performer at Mickey Finn's. He says that the baptism-by-fire experience of that room prepped him for a career in comedy. "You'd have people getting drunk. I had a light explode on me one time. Another time a fight broke out in the corner during my set," he recalls. "But being in that kind of environment gives you a tough skin. When Tom Arnold called me years later and asked if I could read a line in a sitcom, it was no big deal. I wasn't afraid of anything because I had done Mickey Finn's."

Despite the combustible elements inside his bar, Billings remained at arm's length, instructing Gerbino to handle things. "We used to call him the Comedy Colonel," Gerbino says of Billings. "He didn't want to hear about whatever problems people were having; he just wanted us to deal with it so he didn't have to."

In addition to having to navigate the tense relationship between the bar's regulars and the comedy fans, Gerbino and friends also had to contend with the growing number of personalities onstage each night. "Straight across the stage there was a hallway where the emcee would sit," says Hansen. "So that's where you'd have comics whispering about who was taking too much time onstage or who was pissing off whom that night."

Adds Gerbino: "Sometimes you'd get a guy who just wouldn't shut up. We'd be mumbling to each other, 'Get me a match or something to get his attention.' But then you'd try, and they didn't give a shit. Then other nights we'd have guys get up and promise they could do twenty or thirty minutes, and they'd do twelve. They'd walk offstage and all of us would be like, 'Hey thanks, asshole,' because now we had to figure out how to fill an extra fifteen or twenty minutes, when we barely had enough material to do our own sets."

More comics began to find their footing on the Mickey Finn's stage during this time. People like Dillery, Bradley, Dean Johnson, and

Glenn Tanner were becoming regular performers. Still, Gerbino was the glue that held the shows together. He was welcoming to any aspiring comedian who wanted to ply their craft, but Gerbino snuffed out the free-for-all spirit that had characterized the bar's initial efforts at stand-up. "The whole *Gong Show* crap really hurt these comedians," he says. "I wanted a show that was just pure comedy. We'd have clowns and mimes and shit like that who would come by to get onstage, and I'd tell them to get the fuck out. The circus is down the road."

The idea of "pure comedy" leaves plenty of room for interpretation even today. But back in 1977–78, nothing was considered off-limits when it came to material. Some comics stuck with the squeaky-clean, groan-inducing, jokebook humor, like "What did the banana say to the orange? I find you appealing, but I've got to split." (That joke was actually told on the Mickey Finn's stage, and unfortunately it happened to be on a night when a *Minneapolis Tribune* reporter was on hand to review the show. The joke made it into print as an example of what one might hear at a comedy show, even though it was less than representative of the typical performances.) Other acts focused on impressions or comedy bits as opposed to standard jokes or one-liners. For some, sex, drugs, and politics were all very much in play when they took their turns at the microphone.

Dan Bradley (left) and Jeff Gerbino (right) at Mickey Finn's. (Courtesy of Jeff Gerbino)

A handful of female comedians began to brave the stage at Mickey Finn's as well, though women were expected to fit specific roles in their onstage personas. Gail Matthius, who was a regular in Dudley Riggs's troupe and soon would be cast on *Saturday Night Live*, did an interview with the *Minneapolis Tribune* around the time when Mickey Finn's was building its reputation as a comedy spot. She was candid about the situation. "I think that seeing a woman up on stage throws a lot of people off," Matthius said. "If women try and tell the same jokes as the men have been telling—you know, stuff about sex or with four-letter words in it—the people go, 'What is she? Some sort of street person?' We have to come in vulnerable, like Lily Tomlin, not abrasive."

In the fall of 1978, another aspiring comedian found his way to the stage at Mickey Finn's, altering the course of comedy history in Minnesota and beyond: Louie Anderson.

"I brought my family and friends down to the bar one night and did my three minutes," Anderson recalls of his first time onstage. "I got some laughs and that felt really good, but then when I was done everyone got up and left because my friends were just there to see me. I think that made everybody mad that night, but I came back the next week and signed up, and they let me onstage again. And then I did it again the next week, and the next week, and the next week."

Gerbino quickly recognized that Anderson was the real deal. He was a talented performer, and Gerbino believed he could add something to the club. However, not everyone felt the same way. "I saw talent in Louie, and Scott was insulted by that, but Louie had a better natural personality," Gerbino recalls of Hansen's reaction to Anderson entering the fold. It didn't stem from any perceived lack of talent, but it was one of the first instances of competition emerging between comics. "So I decided we should split the show in half and let Louie host the first half."

"I knew that being the emcee was a way for me to get extra stage time," Anderson remembers. "People don't usually want to be the emcee, because they want to be brought up onstage and introduced and all that stuff, but I was just happy to get as much time as I could."

"Louie was the worst emcee in the world," Hansen says. "Most guys who wanted to emcee wanted to be able to do time without having to recycle material that they'd use in the next show. They can kind of go up and say, 'here's what I'm thinking.' So Louie would come out and just start lecturing people in the front row, and then he'd say 'the next guy I'm going to bring up is really funny,' but then someone in the audience would catch his eye, and he'd be like 'you know what I'm thinking about you?' and next thing you know he's back down on the chair for another twenty minutes. So you'd be getting yourself psyched up and you wouldn't know when you were going on. Some nights the show would be like three hours long."

Even with the addition of Anderson, the number of comics who appeared on the Mickey Finn's stage was still pretty limited, and it was up to the core group of guys to figure out how to fill enough time for a proper show.

"I eventually really gelled with the guys," Anderson remembers. "You had me and Jeff and Scott, and you had Billy Bauer and Alex Cole, and really that was our core group. Honestly, I think there was probably only eight or nine of us who were regularly performing at that time, so we all got a chance to go up and do our material. If we had five or six of us at the bar, then the whole show would go for maybe an hour and a half."

With a solid group of performers and a growing audience, rumblings of money talk started to emerge. This was uncharted territory, especially for Billings, who had initially been drawn to the idea of promoting comedy as a way to bring people into his bar, as opposed to promoting it as a stand-alone commodity.

"I told the guys that I couldn't really afford to pay them, but if they wanted to do a cover charge they were welcome to," says Billings. "I wasn't going to try to charge an admission fee for the bar or anything like that myself. It was too soon, and comedy wasn't really proven yet."

Soon admission to the "club" portion of Mickey Finn's cost a dollar, then two, then three, and eventually patrons would fork over a full five dollars to see live stand-up comedy. "They let Bill handle the door at Mickey Finn's," Cole says. "And he was relentless about packing people into that room. We'd be in that hallway getting ready to perform, and he was always approaching us and demanding that we find more chairs. We'd tell him, 'That's all there is!' and he would tell us to go and grab some chairs from one of the other rooms in the union hall because the people already paid the cover and he wasn't going to give them their money back. And we would find some chairs, and then by the time we got back to standing around waiting for the show to start, Billy would be back demanding more chairs. It was like that every show."

Adds Gerbino, "The one thing I'll give him [Bauer] credit for, because of his crazy, bipolar ballsiness, he was the best guy to collect the money at the door. He was always the one pushing to charge people, and I'd go along with it. The other guys were scared shitless, but I mean we were talking about a fucking dollar here. He was adamant that we could make some money, and that's how we were able to start charging."

As the new decade dawned, the mood at Mickey Finn's started to change as the core group began to see the club as a business rather than just a place to pursue their artistic dreams. "One of the first fights we had was because me and Jeff wanted to make up business cards to hand out around town, telling people about the club," says Hansen. "And Bill refused to chip in. So we got the cards made and they said, 'Friday night emcee: Scott Hansen. Saturday night emcee: Jeff Gerbino.' Bill got all pissed off and wanted to know why we left his name off. When we tried to say it's because he didn't kick in any money, he got all paranoid and thought we were trying to get him out."

This was a sign of things to come, and the infighting among the originals was reaching a boiling point. "The owner was getting sick of the bickering, and he was looking to sell the place," Hansen says of Billings.

While Mickey Finn's was still the A-spot for comedy in town, slowly but surely other bars saw the success the place was having and started to open up to the idea of hosting their own comedy nights. Naturally, the owners of these other bars reached out to the Mickey Finn's gang to run things on their behalf. One such place was a bar called Corks, which had a somewhat-regular weeknight stand-up showcase, held on an evening when Mickey Finn's wasn't open for comedy.

First newspaper ad for the Mickey Finn's comedy shows, 1979

Meanwhile, other venues in town, such as the Carlton Celebrity Room, would occasionally bring in bigger names from the world of comedy. The Mickey Finn's boys were not at that level themselves, although they were fearless when it came to promotion. They proved it one night when they managed to pull in one very, very big name to Corks, which brought them a new level of credibility.

"We'd do shows on Monday nights at this place and get maybe ten, fifteen, twenty people, tops," recalls Hansen. "So one week, Rodney Dangerfield is coming to town to perform at the Carlton Celebrity Ballroom, all week, beginning on Tuesday. On Monday afternoon, we made a call to the club to see if we could get ahold of Rodney. They put us in touch with his PR people, and we said, 'Can you tell Rodney that we'd like to invite him to come out to see our show on Monday? We have a great comedy show nearby, and we hope he can make it.' Rodney got the message, and he calls us back and says, 'I'm going to come to your show tonight.'" To make sure the room would be full, they called everyone they knew and told them Rodney Dangerfield was coming.

"Sure enough," Hansen continues, "he showed up right on time, and the place was packed. Rodney sat right in the middle of the audience. That night, it was me, Alex, Jeff, and Louie, and we each did twenty minutes. I went on last, and just as I'm wrapping up, I look at Rodney and he quietly points at himself, as if to say he'd like to do some time. Of course I'm going to let him do whatever he wants, so I say, 'Ladies and gentlemen, Rodney Dangerfield.' He comes up and does forty-five minutes on our little stage. It was unreal. He signed every autograph he was asked for. He talked to the four of us for as long as we wanted to talk. He was just a great guy."

Dangerfield also stopped by Mickey Finn's as a fan later on to check on the group and offer some words of advice for how to keep growing. Once word got out that an A-list star had provided his stamp of approval to Mickey Finn's core group of comics, the club's reputation—as well as that of the original five of Gerbino, Hansen, Bauer, Cole, and Anderson—exploded locally and beyond. Mickey Finn's was anointed as the place to go to see "real" comedy, and more big names from out of town began to seek out the club as a place to hone their act.

"We had Joan Rivers come through. Tiny Tim performed at Mickey Finn's. And Jeff really gets the credit for that," remembers Anderson. "He was the one who was always pushing us to do more and build on what we were doing."

Gerbino was clearly the best networker in the group. He would introduce himself to any and all comics who came through town or whom he met on the rare road gig. His bravado and confidence were both a selling point and a challenge for out-of-towners to come to the bar.

"You'd get these performers on the road who would brag about how they came up through the hard New York comedy scene,"

Jeff Gerbino and Rodney Dangerfield at Mickey Finn's. (Courtesy of Jeff Gerbino)

Gerbino says. "I'd snap back, 'You're playing boutique comedy clubs. What's hard about that? I'm in the basement of a union bar where they don't even want us.' That would get their attention, hearing that some Irish-Italian kid from New York was hosting a show in Minneapolis. All of a sudden they'd say, 'I didn't know you guys had a comedy scene,' and it was enough to get them out here to check it out."

By 1980, comedy was booming both locally and nationally. The increased interest in comedy through late-night talk shows and stand-up specials led to an increase in people flocking to see live comedy in their own backyard, and Mickey Finn's was reaping the benefits. However, with more and more comedy fans showing up on a regular basis, it was apparent the gang needed to widen the talent pool.

Joel Madison and Jeff Cesario are two of the most accomplished comedy writers and comics ever to come out of Minnesota. Madison created the hit sitcom *Malcolm & Eddie* in the 1990s and wrote episodes for several other high-profile sitcoms, and he continues to write in Hollywood today. Cesario is still a touring comedian who has won two Emmy Awards for his writing on *The Larry Sanders Show* and *The Dennis Miller Show*. But before all that, they were two kids looking to get stage time at Mickey Finn's.

"Mickey Finn's was getting return crowd members, but they were getting the same acts quite a bit," recalls Cesario. "The performers were just doing their acts because they were responsible for filling a good thirty or thirty-five minutes each per night. But the audiences were like, 'Hey, you got any new comics?' Then they saw these two kids Joel Madison and Jeff Cesario who were just writing their wieners off. We'd come in every week with fifteen minutes of new comedy, so they'd let us go up and do our stuff."

Adds Madison, "We learned so much from those guys back then, and that was so helpful. Watching those guys was all the education you needed to do comedy."

Anderson, who was quickly becoming the breakout star of the group, recognized the talent the two comedians brought to the stage and encouraged them to become regular performers. "Louie told me that if I ever wanted stage time I should come down on the weekend," says Cesario. "He goes, 'You won't make any money because no one makes any money, but if you're interested you should keep coming back.' And I was, so I did."

As the scene at Mickey Finn's was growing and more and more performers were coming in to get stage time, another element was beginning to influence the scene: drugs and alcohol.

"I had a new act that I scheduled for later on in the show one night," Gerbino remembers. "Then I spent the whole night watching him sit at the bar drinking anything he could get his hands on. By the time he was on, he could hardly stand up."

New comics drinking to calm their nerves before taking the stage may have been relatively harmless, but drugs were becoming a bigger issue, with Bauer being the most notorious abuser of the group. "We all experimented," Gerbino says. "But Bill was on a whole other level."

Bauer's use and the general drug culture of the time was something of a turnoff for Hansen, who was already having his frustrations with the group. "There were a lot of drugs going on down there. Really hard-core shit. Like people passing out from needles and stuff," Hansen recalls. "I wasn't that straight at the time, but I couldn't deal with all that."

It also had become fairly well known within the comedy circle that Bauer was shorting patients' medications in his job as a paramedic. One person who was around the scene at the time but asked not to be named says that Hansen was the one who ultimately made the call that got Bauer fired from his job: "Bill was saying that he gave patients however many milliliters of morphine or whatever, and then he was doing the rest himself. And still working. He did that for years. Scott tries to play the saint, but he was the one who called and turned in Bill to the hospital. That's why he lost his job, and that's why they had the big falling out."

Yelling, arguing, and the occasional tussle might have been common as tempers and emotions flared among the group (Gerbino recalls a night when he and Bauer went outside to handle a misunderstanding; to this day, he won't reveal the outcome), but an incident involving drugs, kids, and paranoia pushed things over the edge.

"My sister called me and said she saw a van that belonged to a friend of Bill's at the junior high school near St. Francis," Hansen recalls. "And that he was selling drugs to kids. The next time I saw Bill at the bar, I approached him because I wanted to know if he was aware and if he had anything to do with it. Before I could finish, he decided that I had turned him in to the police. Keep in mind, at this point no one had talked with anyone, let alone turned anyone in. But he was so paranoid from all the drugs that you couldn't reason with him."

Although Hansen claims the two of them never actually came to blows, others heard a different account of the event. While he wasn't there that evening, Madison recalls hearing that when all the commotion went down, Gerbino and Anderson prevented anyone else from witnessing the incident. "Me and Jeff [Cesario] heard that they wouldn't let anyone downstairs when the yelling started," Madison says. "Apparently Bill got Scott in a headlock and dragged him up the stairs and out of the building, which shows you how much rage he had to have because dragging Scott Hansen anywhere is no easy task."

Physical encounters aside, Gerbino says that Hansen's growing sense of resentment escalated his reaction and ultimately led to the breakup of the original five.

"It had gotten crazy," Gerbino says. "Jealousy had taken over. So when Bill and Scott got into their fight, Scott got terribly emotional. He's telling me that Bill's the problem and all this, and in that moment, honestly, Bill seemed like the more reliable of the two. I just stood there and told him, 'You need to cool off, and coming down here three times a week isn't the way to do it.' Looking back, I could have handled it better, but I was twenty-four or twenty-five years old, so it was the best I could do."

Hansen left that night and never returned to Mickey Finn's. The bar would continue to run shows for a few more years, and new comedians still found their footing on the makeshift stage. But Hansen's departure signaled the end of the original Mickey Finn's run.

Billings eventually sold the bar to a new owner, who brought changes that the remaining members of the original five weren't too excited about. "Billings sold it to some jerk named Jimmy Andresak, I believe his name was," recalls Gerbino. "His idea of a comedy promotion was to have a raffle for a bottle of booze."

So they decided to look for new stages beyond Mickey Finn's to showcase their talents, including a nearby place called the Varsity Club. Gerbino continues: "We found this great location called the Varsity Club in the University Dinkytown area. I had heard about it before but never took action since it was so close to Finn's. But once most of us left Finn's, I was open to trying it."

Along with Gerbino, longtime Mickey Finn's vets like Rocky Johnson, Dan Bradley, and even Gerbino's old rival Gary Johnson wound up choosing places like the Varsity Club and other new stages that were popping up around town, rivaling Mickey Finn's as a destination for patrons looking for a laugh and new performers looking to cut their teeth in front of a live audience. These places were excited to try out comedy, based on the groundswell it was generating locally, but not many were interested in investing fully in comedy, like Finn's had done. "I think the Varsity became a running shoe store or something," Gerbino says. "I know if they would have stuck with comedy and I would have stayed, that place would have had a good run."

In time, the performers would find other new stages or, in Hansen's case, begin managing clubs and creating stages for comics. But without the little basement dive bar in Northeast, none of that would have ever come to fruition.

In the grand scheme of things, Mickey Finn's burned hot and flamed out relatively quickly as a comedy club. Still, much in the way

Mickey Finn's newspaper ad, 1980

that athletes look back on early days of pickup games with friends or musicians talk about jamming at parties, Mickey Finn's was the place where countless comedians began to find their voices, and where a new comedy scene launched itself to the next level.

"Those first few years, they were a real time of learning," Gerbino recalls fondly. "It's like when you're a freshman in college compared to when you're a senior. You're a lot more confident when you're a senior than when you're a freshman. That's what Mickey Finn's allowed us to do. We could grow up."

··· 2 ···

The Original Five

Finding stand-up comedians anywhere outside of New York or Los Angeles back in the late 1970s was next to impossible. Just ask Jeff Gerbino.

"A comedian was about as rare as an astronaut," Gerbino says of the early days of the Twin Cities comedy scene. "I might as well have been in a space suit. That's how rare it was."

In fact, by Gerbino's estimation, there were maybe three hundred comedians in the entire country during his first few years of performing, including everything from casual comics who were just pursuing a hobby all the way to seasoned pros who had dreams of making it to television. "I knew about all of them," he says.

Even more rare than finding a comic in those days was finding a *talented* comic. Yet somehow, the original five of Gerbino, Hansen, Bauer, Anderson, and Cole were all incredible talents in their own right.

Alex Cole was the performer. Getting his start in improv, Cole was the first of the five to try performing on a regular basis. He told jokes, did impressions, played guitar, and sang. Cole was known for being an incredible storyteller, as well as someone who knew how to write a great story.

Scott Hansen was the "punny" guy. He was a talented writer who knew how to connect with audiences on a level that was approachable and easy to digest. His jokes were clever, and he was able to string together premises effortlessly while maintaining a (mostly) clean repertoire of jokes.

The original five: (clockwise from top left) Louie Anderson, Jeff Gerbino, Scott Hansen, Alex Cole, and Bill Bauer at Mickey Finn's. (Courtesy of Jeff Gerbino)

Jeff Gerbino was the tough guy. His gruff New York attitude gave him an edge, and his material was more focused on politics and current events than the others' more family-friendly jokes.

Louie Anderson was the likeable one. Not that they each didn't have their charms, but Anderson had a way of connecting with a crowd on the fly and making the audience feel like the show he was performing was designed especially for them. He was warm and loveable and could play in front of any audience.

And Bill Bauer was the wild card. He was the darkest among his peers, digging deep into the depths of his mind and pulling out the grossest, most controversial and uncomfortable bits of comedy that most audiences had seen or heard.

While each of the five had his own distinct style, they couldn't have complemented each other better.

Joel Madison and Jeff Cesario had the opportunity to learn from all five during their days trying to break into comedy, and they gained something special from each of them. "Alex was already big time by the time everyone else was just getting started. He had an agent and a lawyer, he had money, he wore this duster around that looked really cool, and he was opening for rock bands," says Madison. "All you had to do was watch Alex Cole and you learned how to do stand-up comedy."

"Louie Anderson was the most amazing, natural talent maybe I've ever seen," he continues. "He could work a crowd like nobody I've ever seen. Still to this day, he's the best. He knew how to talk to people, how to tie people together. He was a genius."

Gerbino was on his way to Los Angeles around the time Madison entered the scene, but the younger comic was able to learn from him as well. "He was very New York, kind of harsh, a little tougher than the rest."

Cesario calls Scott Hansen a "premise bonfire." "That motherfucker would light through jokes about everything, so he'd get through fifty premises in a twenty-minute set. Scott Hansen could write jokes like crazy," he adds.

"And then Bill Bauer, oh god, he was our Sam Kinison. Bill Bauer was a bona fide gonzo comedian," continues Cesario. "He went to premises and places that none of us would think of organically, ever. Bill just went there naturally. He was probably, just in terms of pure comedy, the greatest artist of the group. You'd watch a guy like Bill Bauer and you'd realize this was an art form as much as a craft if you kept your nose to the grindstone."

Similarly, despite their ups and downs and personal issues, each of the five recognized the others' qualities, and how each one's abilities complemented the rest.

"Scott was a great writer," says Anderson. "He did great puns and funny things like that. Just very Minnesota-oriented. Jeff was a New Yorker all the way, just really hard hitting and fast paced. Bill Bauer was a wild man, and Alex Cole was like an actor up there. You'd watch him working out a bit, and he had this tremendous ability to lull you into his comedy."

Anderson says the camaraderie was strong early on, and the group was focused on a common goal: to be the best comics they could be.

Hansen is equally complimentary of the group. "We were all very different, which is what helped us be able to work so cohesively in the beginning," he recalls. "Bill was very off the wall. At times he would downright insult a full audience. Alex Cole, he was a college comic and fluffy as hell, never said a bad word. Gerbino was from New York, and he had impressions and was a little more acerbic. Then I came out and told Minnesotans how different they were."

Cole, too, believes that each comic was talented, but he also notes some of their shortcomings. "You could tell right away who had chops," he recalls. "I was already a pro, but you look at Scott and could tell that he was a great writer who had really good structure. Gerbino, still to this day I think because he's such an asshole human being he didn't make it, but he could have been Bill Maher. He was a brilliant political comedian and had the classic New York look. Watching him work was incredible. Billy Bauer I never thought was going to make it. When I first saw him, I thought, 'He makes me laugh, but he's just too fucking crazy and too dark.' But that son of a bitch kept working it, and then I eventually got it and got what he was doing. So that was fun to watch. And then Louie is Louie. He's one of the few acts in the history of comedy—and I'm talking the fucking history—who would have been funny in any decade. There are very few acts you can put in any era and know they would kill. I loved watching him."

The group pushed each individual to become a better performer. They occasionally fought each other as individuals, but they all recognized that they were stronger collectively than they were on their own. And, at the start anyway, they genuinely enjoyed each other's company.

"Hansen was always booking road shows for us early on," recalls Cole. "So all of us would pile into a van and head to Duluth or Mankato or someplace like that for a one-night show. It was really old-school style and really fun to do as a bunch of young and fearless performers. We were just making it up as we went."

Hansen recalls another road trip with the gang. "Me, Louie, and Gerbino were taking a trip to Chicago, and Louie gets stopped for a speeding ticket," he says. "None of us have cash, none of us have checkbooks, and none of us have credit cards. At that time, you had to pay a bond for a speeding ticket on the spot. So the cop follows us for twenty miles into this small town to get some money, and we manage to scrape together eighty dollars or whatever it was. I think I was the one who came up with most of the cash, but that was fine. So we get to Louie's sister's house, where we were staying for the night, and we crash in the basement. I wake up in the middle of the night, and there's Louie and Gerbino playing cards. They're playing poker against each other and neither will let the other one quit, and they just keep passing money back and forth. They didn't have any money when it came time for us to pay that ticket, but they suddenly had money to play poker."

Despite Anderson and Gerbino's late-night poker game, the trio did a show the following night, and sure enough, back at Louie's sister's house afterward, the two of them were at it again, playing poker into the wee hours of the morning. With both Anderson and Gerbino completely dead tired, things got a little punchy on the drive back to Minnesota. "Louie had found this little plastic figurine along the way that had lost its head," Hansen recalls. "He's sitting there messing around with it, and he goes, 'I'm thinking about getting an aquarium and naming my guy 'Water-Head.' What do you think about that?' And we couldn't stop laughing. He was completely serious. I mean we wouldn't stop making fun of him for miles and miles and miles. We kept bringing it up and bringing it up, and Louie's getting madder and madder, and finally he goes, 'Pull the car over! I'm going to kill both of you guys!'"

While picking at each other on the road was common among the comedians, the debauchery often went up a notch when Bauer was in the mix, such as one night when Hansen, Gerbino, and Bauer did a show in St. Cloud. "We get to the venue," Hansen recalls, "and they've got this little bar set up. So I went to the bar and got a beer, and the guy tells me that performers drink for free. I go back and sit down, and Bill asks me, 'Where'd you get that?' I point him to the little window and tell him that performers drink for free. Next thing I know, here comes Bill carrying a full tray of beers. He sits down and we're looking at him, and I ask, 'Did you get beers for everyone?' and without even a smile he goes, 'No, I did not,' and proceeds to drink the entire tray by himself. About half an hour later I went back up to the bar, and the rules had changed. Performers no longer drank for free thanks to Bill."

Of course, when you put very talented individuals with similar goals together, the competitive juices are bound to flow. That was no different with the original five. "I was never competitive with my stand-up, but the rest of the guys were competitive as hell," remembers Anderson. "But that's healthy. I think comedy is sports in some ways, and you've got to be in shape to do it. I just always thought I was the best one."

Adds Hansen, "We were all very competitive. We were competitive for time, and we were competitive to control the stage. We'd all be doing a show together, and you'd have the five of us arguing over who was going to close the show. I'd tell Jeff, 'I'll go on after you, but you better not do this bit or that bit.' Of course we were [competitive], but that's also how we made each other better."

At Jeff Gerbino's wedding: (from left) Scott Hansen, Gerbino, Louie Anderson, and Alex Cole. (Courtesy of Jeff Gerbino)

Tom Hansen, Scott's brother, spent quite a bit of time with the original five later on when he was helping Scott manage his clubs. Tom says he saw the competition grow firsthand, but each man's unique point of view helped ensure that things stayed mostly friendly. "You could see the rivalries and the jealousy between the guys, especially Alex, Bill, and Scott when they were all together," Tom says. "The thing is, Alex had a lot of success on the college market, Bill had success as a writer out in LA, Scott had success running the clubs, and Louie had success as a performer. Everyone had his own niche. They picked on each other pretty hard, but then they'd get together and have drinks and play cards after."

Eventually time, money, proximity, and competition would affect their relationships, but Cole says their shared desire to put on the best show possible always won out.

"The show must go on, that's something us old guys had in us," he says. "We could be fighting or arguing about something, but we'd think, 'God dammit, it's eight o'clock. Let's rock this house.' It was fun."

··· 3 ···

Jeff Gerbino

When he started hosting weekly comedy shows at Mickey Finn's, Jeff Gerbino would open with the line: "My name is Jeff Gerbino, and I'm not responsible for what goes on here."

That line may have been good for a laugh, but in reality, Gerbino was entirely responsible for Mickey Finn's even having a comedy show. He was the master of ceremonies, the head of marketing, the talent coordinator, and in some cases, the crowd control. In other words, he was the glue that held it all together.

Before he was helping to build the Twin Cities comedy scene from the ground up, Gerbino was a kid from New York who wanted to be on TV. "The first time I ever heard about stand-up comedy is when I was living in New York," he recalls. "It was a story in the paper about the Improv, which was pretty much the only comedy club in the world. The journalist who wrote about it must have come down late or picked a bad night. He wrote about how all the comics bombed, how they went on late, and just how it was a bad experience. I found out later that there were plenty of really great acts and people who would make a big impact in comedy there that night. But I read that and was kind of intimidated about the whole thing."

Without stand-up comedy as a viable option for a career, Gerbino chose to focus his attention on breaking into radio and television. Around that same time, he and his brother decided to make a move to Minnesota. "I moved here for a woman, which is something you should never do," Gerbino says with a laugh. "But I also came out here because New York was a big, intimidating place, so I figured I might have a better chance in Minnesota."

Gerbino enrolled in a local broadcasting school and quickly jumped into that world. "I used to joke when we moved here that I was going to end up working in a cornfield," he recalls. "Sure enough, my first [broadcasting] job was in River Falls [in Wisconsin] next to a cornfield. Some people I went to school with made fun of me for it, but I looked at it like, 'I got a job two months after graduating and they were still unemployed so who's laughing at who?'"

While Gerbino was putting his voice and comedy talents to use on the radio airwaves, his brother got a job managing a print shop in St. Cloud. Though they worked in different places, they remained close, and Gerbino credits his brother for being his number one fan and supporter. "It was always important to me to make my brother laugh," Gerbino remembers.

Around this time, Gerbino began dabbling in comedy wherever he could find an opportunity for stage time, although stage time was fairly limited. "Back then they didn't have comedy shows," he recalls. "They had these fucking gong shows that were basically the medieval equivalent of comedy shows. We'd be trying to slide in a joke in between people singing that 'Johnny B. Goode' song five fucking million times."

Finally, Gerbino and his brother cooked up an idea. They knew Jeff had the talent, but trying to piggyback his way onto someone else's stage wasn't going to provide him with the opportunity he needed. He needed a showcase of his own.

The brothers got in touch with the Grand Mantel Saloon in downtown St. Cloud and convinced the owner to let Gerbino perform a one-night-only comedy show. The bar owner agreed, and the brothers held nothing back when it came to promotion. "We used the print shop my brother worked at to print up all these posters," Gerbino recalls. "We made posters that said, 'New York comedian and impressionist Jeff Gerbino!' and put them all over town. We packed the place, and that night when I got onstage, they were ready for me to be a star. And I was ready to be a star too. And I killed."

For any new or first-time comedian, it sounds like a dream scenario. But for Gerbino, that wasn't the case. "There's nothing worse than killing your first time out," he says. "It's fool's gold. It gives you this false sense of confidence. Plus, at that point there was nowhere else for me to perform and nothing else for me to do. But I knew that I wanted to perform and that if I could stay close to the media working like I was, there would be an opportunity to hook those together."

That opportunity came in the form of an advertisement he saw for a comedy competition at Mickey Finn's. Though Gerbino wasn't exactly sure what he was getting into, the idea of a show that was just comedy was enough to get him through the doors and onto the stage.

Not long after the ten-week contest wrapped and he was asked to take the reins of the comedy night at Mickey Finn's, Gerbino says he knew he had to focus not only on being a performer but on nurturing an entire comedy scene. "I came from a place where performers weren't nurtured—unless you wanted to be nurtured into the ground. So when I started telling people about this little dingy bar in Minneapolis that was doing comedy with some New York guy running the show, I had to really build it up and let people know—or at least make them believe—it was something special."

That was easier said than done. At that time, neither comedians nor fans had much familiarity with stand-up, and it was particularly difficult to get their heads around the concept of a full night devoted to it. "Most people had never seen anything beyond just five minutes of comedy on *The Tonight Show*," he recalls. "If I wasn't so young and brash and full of hubris, I don't know what would have happened."

As he was digging in on the comedy, Gerbino left his radio position and took a job as an auto parts salesman as a way to pay the bills. However, after he was laid off from the job in March 1978, he decided to dedicate himself fully to comedy.

"I never took another civilian job in my life," he says proudly. "That's one thing I was always able to say. Other acts would come to town or I'd do shows in other places, and I'd be able to say that I made my living as a comedian. Well, I wasn't exactly making a living, but I was getting paid. It wasn't $100 million like a basketball player or something, but doing comedy and supporting myself felt like $100 million to me."

His work ethic matched his dedication. Gerbino became a comedy machine. He was pursuing every opportunity to get onstage while still working tirelessly to build up Mickey Finn's reputation as a comedy destination. "I had to really get out there and find places to perform. You had to solicit opportunities back then," he says. "I'd occasionally get calls for different things, and a lot of times they were inappropriate places for comedy, but I knew I had to get onstage. I had to perform. I even did weddings a few times, which were the worst places I've ever performed. The bride and groom would like me, but none of the people at the wedding would. It was awful, but I went wherever there were opportunities."

Gerbino also tapped into his media background to gain traction in the local press. "I'd get more press than the traveling comedians who were coming to town," he says. "Not because I was better, but because I understood radio and was able to perform in a way that was best for them."

He landed a regular spot on WCCO radio in Minneapolis, which was a huge score for any performer looking to drum up publicity during that time. "I was the first comedian to get on WCCO, and that was a big deal back then," he recalls. "It was basically like when people switched off WCCO for the night, the lights went off [throughout the state]. It was that big of a deal in people's lives. So I would get regular spots with them, and all of a sudden people up in Stearns County [northwest of the Twin Cities] knew who I was because they would get the station up there. Pretty soon, [WCCO] started letting me do some fill-in shifts on the air when someone would get sick, so that was a big boost for me."

Gerbino knew the station provided solid exposure for him as a performer, but he also understood the importance of using it as a vehicle to grow the comedy scene as a whole. "I was competitive as all fuck," he deadpans. "I could bring other comedians on if they were famous and coming in from out of town, but as far as local comedians it was just me. That said, I still did what was good for comedy and used that to get people to check out all the performers at our shows."

His willingness to help his fellow comedians made Gerbino something of a role model in the scene early on. When the *Minneapolis*

twin cities
Reader
The Newspaper For Young Twin Citians

TAKE THAT, STEVE MARTIN!

Fighting to stay alive on the Twin Cities comedy circuit p. 5

Jeff Gerbino

Volume 3 Issue 8   Friday, March 3, 1978

Jeff Gerbino on the cover of the Twin Cities Reader, *1978*

Tribune did a feature on Mickey Finn's in the fall of 1978, it spot-lighted Gerbino as the unofficial local leader and the protector of new performers.

"I don't want a heckler going after these acts, especially the new ones," Gerbino told the paper. This was a commendable and unen-viable position for a young man in his early twenties to put himself in, all while trying to find his own path as a comic. "I still remember my first heckler—the fear that it instills in you. I try and stop that if I can."

Providing other comedians with the opportunities for stage time, he says, was the key to turning people on to comedy and helping the performers grow. "I'd give anyone who was funny an opportunity," he says. "They'd ask me for advice or try to endear themselves to me, and I'd just tell them, 'Look, all I've got on you is maybe six months of performing. I'm trying to figure this all out the same as you are.'"

Also in the *Tribune* article, Gerbino took time away from promot-ing the club and his own budding comedy career to talk up his fel-low performers and the environment they created at Mickey Finn's. "The acts have really improved," he said. "They come down here to learn and they are learning quite a bit. A group of us went down to appear at a similar club in Milwaukee recently, and we discovered they were about five million light years behind us."

As a performer, Gerbino was making major strides. He was less planful onstage than some of the others, more intellectual and quick on his feet. His material was more sophisticated and faster paced than that of any of the other original five, and he was the most po-litically charged. But he was also a tremendous impressionist, work-ing characters into his act that ranged from Howard Cosell to Kmart clerks and Iron Rangers.

His PR savvy and his talent combined to make Gerbino arguably the hottest commodity in local comedy for a time, and he was invited to perform as an opening act for musicians who came to town. "I opened for Natalie Cole, and it was great," he recalls. "The crowd was very nice and polite. Then I opened for Steve Miller Band, and it absolutely sucked. I'd get up there and nobody knew who I was, and nobody cared. But back then, those were prized gigs, and it's how I was scraping together a living."

Even after the fight between Bill Bauer and Scott Hansen that spurred the fracturing of the original five, Gerbino continued to run the comedy shows at Mickey Finn's for a little while longer, before ultimately deciding to pack up and move to California. But first he planted a seed for the next chapter of Twin Cities comedy.

"I told Louie [Anderson] that he needed to go talk to Dudley Riggs," Gerbino says. "The guys who were left—Bill and Alex Cole—he wasn't going to be able to hang around with those guys. He wasn't into drugs at all, and it wasn't going to work if he wanted to keep performing and keep getting better."

Gerbino experienced some success in Los Angeles, but, he admits, his time in the Twin Cities had spoiled him. "I was used to early success," he says. "When I got to LA, it was like, 'Okay, you're a comic. What's the big deal?' Just the jadedness of it all was tough."

Gerbino eventually returned to the Twin Cities, as both a radio personality and a comedian, building on his already notable place in local comedy history. While he may never have achieved major fame or fortune, the kid who started making a living in comedy when there were no clubs and no structure was able to maintain that life well into his retirement years.

"Not a lot of guys can say they were a successful middle-class comic," he says. "Would I have liked to have been massively famous? Hell, yeah. But I'm happily retired and don't have to work another day in my life thanks to comedy. And to me, that's pretty impressive."

4

Bill Bauer

While his peers were focused on puns and clean comedy, Bill Bauer went darker with his jokes. Much darker.

Minneapolis Star staff writer Karin Winegar stopped in to Mickey Finn's one night in the late seventies to get a look at this burgeoning comedy scene. While others were lauded for their ability to keep the audience rolling, Bauer was singled out by Winegar as a "vomic" who "produces frighteningly weird, sexist, racist material." Taste in comedy is always subjective, but his fellow comedians agree that pandering to the audience was not something Bauer was concerned with.

"There was one night where Bill was supposed to do twenty minutes, and he ended up doing forty," recalls Louie Anderson. "I was getting mad at him for going long, so when he got offstage I said, 'Bill, you were supposed to do twenty minutes and you did forty.' He said to me, 'They made me eat it for twenty minutes, so I wanted them to eat it for twenty minutes.'"

Offstage, Bauer was known for being a loose cannon who loved to party and wasn't afraid of the consequences. That's probably what earned him the nickname "Wild Bill."

Sadly, Bauer passed away in 2012 at the age of sixty-two. He was survived by his wife, Cheryl, who has since passed, and his son, Patrick, who was born in 1978 just as Bauer was getting his feet wet with comedy. Although Patrick was too young to experience his father's formative comedy years, Bill shared his journey with his son, and Patrick has followed in his footsteps.

Bill Bauer onstage at Mickey Finn's in 1980. (Courtesy of Craig Allen)

"He wasn't as conventional as some of his peers," Patrick says of his father. "He always said he wasn't really a great joke writer in the beginning. He would just say a lot of shocking things onstage, but he had a funny way of saying them."

Before making his way to comedy, Bauer served in Vietnam. Upon returning home to Minnesota, he worked as a used car salesman and, later, as a paramedic. Unlike some of the other originals, Bauer never had dreams of performing comedy as a young boy, nor had he grown up devouring comedy albums or television performances. He kind of just stumbled into it.

"He had a lot of horror stories about being a paramedic," Patrick says. "It's a job where you see a lot of bad stuff. People would say that's why he had a dark sense of humor. But honestly, that's just who he was. So when he heard there was a place to do comedy, he decided, why not?"

While the stage offered a new place to showcase his personality, Bauer was the same guy in private as he was in front of crowds. A longtime friend of Bauer's, Michael Valentini, worked with Bauer as an ambulance driver. He told a story to a local newspaper after Bauer's passing about how his partner had once fallen asleep on the job at the ambulance quarters and was jolted awake by an emergency call. Bauer jumped up and sped off to the patient's house. When he arrived, he walked in with no hat, his red tie hanging open, a wrinkled shirt and pants, and no shoes. "Wild Bill" wasn't just a nickname; it was the way he lived his life.

After a few appearances at Mickey Finn's, Bauer connected with Jeff Gerbino, who decided to bring him into his inner circle, along with Scott Hansen. But unlike Hansen or Gerbino, who saw comedy as an art form and a business opportunity, Bauer was more focused on the lifestyle of hard drinking, drugs, and making people squirm.

"There was one night that Bauer walks into the club carrying a fucking nitrous oxide tank that he'd stolen from his job as a paramedic," Gerbino recalls. "I'm just staring at him like, 'What the fuck are you gonna do with that?' and he just smiled and goes, 'The fuck do you think?'"

Another night, Bauer and a few other comics had done a generous amount of cocaine before his set. When he stepped onstage to begin his act, he heard something he hadn't anticipated: complete silence.

The other guys he was partying with, including Alex Cole and his brother Danny, could hear Bauer onstage but were surprised to hear no one laughing. When they looked up from their drinks and conversation, they noticed that Bauer had blood pouring out of his nose, as if he had just been in a brutal accident. Danny, recognizing that the very intoxicated Bauer had no clue why he was being met with stunned silence from the audience, went running over with a dishrag. He wiped his friend's face and then showed him the blood-soaked rag. Without missing a beat, Bauer shrugged and said softly into the microphone, 'I haven't seen that much blood since Ali-Frazier!' Suddenly the horror show turned into a punch line, and Bauer took the crowd on a roller coaster of emotions from there.

That may have been one of the more memorable moments involving hard drugs, but it wasn't unusual to see Bauer drink so much that he'd vomit onstage mid-set, only to continue telling jokes without pause.

Beyond his shocking material and hard-partying ways, Bauer's sense of humor was lined with a unique ability to see the world through a slightly different lens. "My dad wasn't making jokes that other people were making," Patrick says. "He wasn't even talking about the same things as anyone else. He was talking about family things, but he'd touch on things like death and more uncomfortable stuff that most people push to the back of their minds."

"We always watched Bill," Anderson said of his late friend. "Even though, in our comedy, we weren't like him, we always wanted to see what he had in store next for the audience, and for us. He was a comic's comic in a lot of ways."

Jeff Cesario may have summed it up best when he said, "Bill Bauer would write a joke because it was crawling inside of him and it had to get out."

Of course, there are also the stories of Bauer coming to blows with pretty much anyone he didn't like at Mickey Finn's, from bar patrons to the infamous fight with Hansen. Anderson calls Bauer the club's "comedy policeman," and he remembers him fondly for his protective, albeit short-tempered approach to looking after his fellow comics. "If you pushed it too far with the heckling or you were being a jerk, Bill would have no problem walking right up to you and grabbing you out of your seat," Anderson recalls.

According to Patrick, those stories fit Bauer's overall temperament. "That is so typical of my old man," Patrick laughs. "If you were a buddy of his, he was great to you. He really tried to be nice to other comics, trying to help people however he could. But if he didn't like you, he could be hard to deal with. Especially when he was younger. Once you were on my dad's shit list, it was pretty fucking hard to get off of it."

Tom Hansen, Scott's younger brother, knew Bauer from a very young age. "I knew Bill Bauer because Scott was best friends with his brother, Tim," recalls Tom. "I knew Bill from the time I was maybe six years old. We would have dinner at their house, we went to the same church. Things like that."

Tom later joined his older brother in the comedy business, first as a ticket-taker before moving up to club manager and a booking agent for comics for road gigs. That's where he saw the other side of Bauer. "Bill was plain crazy," Tom says. "He told my wife, Holly, that he was going to pay to have me killed one time. He goes, 'For $500 I could have your husband knocked off. Tell him to knock off the shit.'"

That might sound a bit extreme, but Tom says death threats were just part of Bauer's charm. "He always had a touch of crazy, which is what made him who he was," Tom continues. "He threatened to kill my brother Scott a few times too. You really weren't on the A-list in local comedy until Bill Bauer threatened to kill you."

As he got older, Bauer was less likely to get into physical altercations, but that didn't mean he had lost his edge. As Patrick recalls, "He told me a story about a time he did a week of shows out of town somewhere, and the club owner burned him. So he booked another week at the club. The day of the first show, he called the guy and goes, 'Hey, it's Bill Bauer. The flight got delayed but I should be there in a little bit.' Then a couple of hours later he calls and says, 'Hey, it's Bill Bauer again. I made it, so I'm grabbing a cab and I'll be over there soon.' Then another hour goes by and he calls again and says, 'Hey, it's Bill Bauer. My cabbie got lost, but I'll make sure I'm there in time.' Then like five minutes before showtime he calls the guy and says, 'Hey, it's Bill Bauer. I'm still at home so why don't you go fuck yourself?' I couldn't believe he did that, but that's what happened when someone crossed him."

Bauer split up with his wife early on in his comedy career, when Patrick was three years old, leaving her to do the majority of the child rearing solo. Patrick would still see his father, but the younger Bauer says Bill wasn't necessarily doing a great job of balancing his comedy aspirations with his parenting responsibilities. "I lived with him for a little while in like fourth grade, but he was gone all the time at that point," Patrick recalls. "But it's not like he was completely absent from my life growing up. I have plenty of fond memories of spending time with him. He wasn't short on love. It's just kind of how it was. But I never felt unloved, so in that way he did a good job."

Despite his short temper, Bauer was known to be just as warm and helpful to his peers as he was to his family, serving as a mentor of sorts to new comics climbing the ranks. "He helped out a lot of people and gave them their start," Patrick shares. "Obviously he helped me when

I was starting out, but he tried to do the same for other people too. There was always somebody new hanging around, and my dad would help them out and give them a guest spot and check them out, and whenever he could he'd pay them, even if it was just twenty bucks for gas. He knew what it was like trying to get started."

It wasn't unusual for Bauer to sit down with a new comic after watching their set and go through their act piece by piece. He wasn't being critical; rather, he would advise them about parts of their act that needed fixing and how to enhance their jokes, and he offered positive encouragement. For the most part. "He could be blunt," Patrick adds with a laugh. "He had no problem telling someone that a joke had been done to death. Or maybe they shouldn't sprinkle in racial epithets. Stuff like that."

Bauer's motivation for helping people and pulling up the underdogs went back to his ever-present anti-establishment attitude. "Part of it was just that the people he didn't like in comedy were greedy assholes and he liked sticking it to them," Patrick recalls. "But I think he just genuinely enjoyed being nice and wanted to do what was good for comedy."

Alex Cole says that Bauer was always looking for the best in every comic. "He had no ego whatsoever," Cole says. "He just wanted to make people laugh."

As the comedy scene continued to evolve, and as new doors began to open for the original five, Bauer made another pivotal life decision. "He quit the drinking and drugs, probably around 1981 or '82," Patrick says. "It's not something that he announced or made a big deal out of, and I don't think a lot of people realized how bad it was, because he wasn't a guy who needed a shot in the morning to get his hands to stop shaking. But when he was out in the club performing, he didn't have an off switch."

That hard-partying lifestyle led to a major crisis in Bauer's career and ultimately altered his trajectory as both a comic and a person. "He never told me what it was, but he said that he blew a big opportunity," Patrick says. "And it must have been pretty big because he realized that the drinking and drugs weren't helping his career, and so he quit."

Bauer turned a corner and became more intent on joke writing and structure and on creating new opportunities for himself. "He focused on becoming a really talented writer and got away from the crazier stuff that he had relied on for a lot of his career," Patrick says. "He started structuring his comedy to have a beginning, a middle, and an end, and that got him to a place where he could perform in more places."

After relocating to Los Angeles in 1987, Bauer would land upward of twenty-five national TV appearances, several of which were on his old friend Louie Anderson's comedy specials. He also did some writing for the sitcom *Roseanne* and even had a bit part in one episode. Although he never made it to *The Tonight Show* or other late-night talk shows like some of his peers, he was able find his way onto some stand-up shows that ran on the early days of MTV, and he became in demand nationally. "My phone rang constantly with people willing to employ me without seeing me," Bauer said in an interview the year before his death.

The man who had once roasted Ann Landers's five questions to determine if you're an alcoholic and made light of taboo topics like drunk driving and even the crucifixion was now getting booked in fancy banquet halls and at corporate gigs. "That part is insane to me," Patrick says. "Because he was this guy who started out being crazy and shocking, and now companies were like, 'This is a guy who should perform at our Christmas party.'"

According to Tom Hansen, however, Bauer's idea of "clean" comedy wasn't always the same as everyone else's. "Bill got mad at me because he thought he could do corporate gigs, and I never put him in corporates," Tom explains, in regard to his role as booking agent. "Bill thought he was a clean comic. The thing is, he didn't swear, but his material was very dark. For example, he had a joke about being raped by a bear. That doesn't fly in the corporate market, where you need to be clean as milquetoast."

As for his relationships with the rest of the original five, Bauer remained close with Anderson up until his death, and he maintained solid professional relationships with Hansen and Gerbino as well. But he was closest to Cole.

"Billy was sort of a best friend to everyone," says Cole. "During my entire time in show business, I was very much of the attitude that if someone told me to do something, I said no. It didn't matter what it was, because I always assumed people had ulterior motives. The only person I would trust was Billy Bauer. He was that good of a person where I knew that if he told me I should do something, I should trust it. On top of that, he always ended up being right."

"I still think of Billy once a week," Cole continues. "I have his picture up on my computer so I can still see him. I used to talk to him every day. I don't have many friends, but Billy was one friend I was really lucky to have."

Bauer's former comrades in comedy all had kind things to say about the wild card of the gang. When the media came calling following Bauer's death in 2012, Anderson summed it up best in a comment in the *St. Paul Pioneer Press*: "Today we lost one of the founding fathers of standup comedy in Minnesota. The funniest guy I ever worked with. He was funny, he was brave, and he was charitable."

That same day, Patrick tweeted something that everyone who had ever encountered Bauer could connect with. "My dad died last week. He'd stated that he was either to be partially cremated or taxidermized. He was awesome, and I love him."

5

Louie Anderson

Beyond a shadow of a doubt, Louie Anderson is the most famous stand-up comedian to come out of Minnesota. He's won Emmy Awards for his animated show, *Life with Louie,* and for his work in the critically acclaimed *Baskets.* He's authored best-selling books, appeared in countless movies and television shows, and performed in front of massive crowds all over the world. But long before Louie Anderson became a megastar, he was a young man who took a dare from a friend.

"I was at Williams Pub [in Uptown Minneapolis] and they were doing a comedy night, and I said to my friend Jim O'Brien, 'I think I'm as funny as these guys are,' and he told me to prove it," Anderson recalls. "I was never going to be a comedian, but I decided to take the dare and go up at Mickey Finn's."

After that fateful night at Mickey Finn's, Anderson was hooked.

As one of eleven children, Anderson grew up around a lot of laughter, as well as quite a bit of pain. Anderson's father was an abusive alcoholic, but he still had love to give. And though not a comedian, his father was an entertainer and would crack open the window that gave Anderson his first look at stand-up comedy. "I was always a kid who watched *The Tonight Show* with my dad," he recalls. "He was a trumpet player and loved Doc Severinsen [former bandleader for the show], so he would let me stay up and watch the comedians. I loved it. I thought they were great, and they made me laugh."

Anderson's mother and father were in the audience that night at

Mickey Finn's, which coincidentally was also the night that a local film crew from PBS was at the bar to film a feature about the new and exciting world of stand-up comedy making its way in Minneapolis. They saw Anderson's set and the crowd reaction and, perhaps somewhat hastily, decided to make him one of the featured faces of the segment.

"Of course that's the night PBS would show up," Jeff Gerbino recalls. "They got all excited and said they wanted to talk to Louie, and we're trying to tell them that the crowd reaction was way out of proportion; it's not real. But they wanted to talk to him and put him on camera. I remember telling them, 'Come back here in a few weeks and see him perform. The reaction will be a lot different.'"

The PBS story did prominently feature Anderson, who at the time was using props, wearing a fake nose and glasses, and incorporating characters into his set. This was a far cry from the more personal material he became known for later in his career, but it was the perfect tone to reach a wider audience, and it quickly established him as the star of the group. That recognition was exactly what he needed to keep going. As he said in the PBS feature, "I started out in comedy to get recognition. I got people's smiles and laughs, and I liked the attention. My approach to comedy is to take everyday situations and blow them out of proportion."

In the same feature, Anderson touched on some of his more painful motivations. "I feel like I'm sharing life experiences that can be shared and understood," he said. "People laugh at some of my jokes because they are laughing not to cry. It's an emotional feeling I get. I like to let people know they aren't the only ones, and I want to hear the laughter so I know I'm not the only one."

Though he had faced difficulties growing up and his relationship with his family was strained at times, Anderson says that his parents were incredibly supportive of his comedy. But after that first night at Mickey Finn's, his family life took another painful turn. "Everyone was so excited and supportive that night, and then the next morning my dad had a stroke," Anderson recalls. "That was a rough blow. You know, you feel a little responsible. He was out that night, he got excited. So that was hard on me. But even after that, everyone was really supportive."

That included Anderson's father himself. "After the stroke he still said to me, 'You can do it, Louie. You'll be great.' He was a thousand percent supportive."

Anderson's difficult upbringing and abusive family environment not only provided fodder for his comedy act; it also drove him to look for work helping children, and he got a job as a childcare expert at a local children's home in St. Paul. "I had a rough childhood, so I identified with that," he explains. "There's a lot of mental illness in my family, and I thought it was a good thing to be helpful. It was something I could do and something I was good at. I got in some trouble when I was a kid, and I had a great probation officer. I had someone who really cared about me and helped me to get back in school and turn my life around."

For a while, Anderson split his time between social work and comedy, pulling from both experiences equally. "Whenever you're dealing with people, whether it's an audience or in a counseling or therapy situation, you're dealing with two sides of the same coin," Anderson says. "Stuff that can be really upsetting and sad can also be hysterical. Tragedy and comedy are just so close together that sometimes they go hand in hand. The only thing you can do is laugh about it."

At a certain point, though, Anderson realized it wasn't plausible to maintain both his social work and comedy careers, so he decided to go all in on the comedy. "The unfortunate thing is that there is no money in social work, and at that time there was even less money in comedy," he says. "Comedy was an all-in-one thing. You don't get paid until you make it, and you don't make it unless you jump in fully. I got so much joy out of social work, but I had so much more of a knack for the comedy than the social work. I was already getting onstage three or four nights a week, so I decided to just dive in completely and take a leap of faith. I never looked back."

Ask any comic about Anderson and they'll be quick to sing his praises for being someone who can write onstage—meaning he can play off the audience and create new material on the fly. "He's better at improvisation than the straight material," says Gerbino. "He's better talking to somebody and ricocheting ideas off that. In all my years, he's one of the best I've ever seen when it comes to playing with an audience. I'd watch him come up with things onstage that were just incredible."

Jeff Cesario echoes this assessment of Anderson's skills as an in-the-moment kind of guy when it came to writing. "A lot of times when you say someone writes onstage, it's a nice way of saying they're lazy," he says with a laugh. "But Louie really did. He could get up and just work the crowd. He could start the month with nothing, and by the end of the month he'd have a killer ten-minute bit about the zoo that didn't exist the first week, all because he met someone one night who worked at the zoo."

Gerbino remembers one night at Mickey Finn's when Anderson's on-the-fly audience interactions took a dark turn, however. "Louie wasn't into drugs, but I saw him go up onstage buzzed a few times. It's like he became his father," says Gerbino. "There was someone in the front row, and I don't know what the guy said or did, but Louie just started railing on him. And it was funny, don't get me wrong. But he'd go back into his emceeing for a few minutes, then sit back

Louie Anderson onstage. (Photo by David Brewster, Minneapolis Star and Tribune, *from the Minnesota Historical Society Collections)*

down on the stool and attack [this guy] again. Eventually the audience was just kind of like, 'Okay, we get it.' When he came offstage that night, he asked me if I thought he went too far. So I told him, 'It was funny for the first ten minutes, but you went twenty-five.' He honestly didn't even realize. He goes, 'I did?' I think that's why he quit alcohol too."

Anderson doesn't remember that specific moment, but he concedes that his upbringing did instill some anger inside of him. "When you're a fat kid, you get picked on," he says. "My dad was a very tough guy, very abusive. So I had this whole catalog of abuse to unleash on somebody if they hassled me. I could be just terrible. But the thing is, every time I'd shut someone down if they were mean to me, I always felt terrible. My comedy comes from a place of love, and I wanted to use it to make people happy."

So he decided to stick to his clean, family-friendly comedy. One evening, he received a piece of advice from another comedian that stuck with him and became a turning point in his career. "There was a comedian named Roman Dicaire," Anderson recalls. "One night I came offstage, and I had been doing material about my family. He said, 'If you do that family stuff, and you do a clean act, you'll become famous, Louie.' For some reason I believed he was right, so I kept doing clean material. I never swore or anything like that."

Anderson worked hard at honing his act. Every night he would record his set on a handheld cassette player and then listen to it on his drive home. As he built his act as well as a local following, he also began mentoring other up-and-coming comedians, including a woman named Priscilla Nelson.

"I became really good friends with Louie, and we'd all go out after shows sometimes," Nelson recalls. "All of the comedians who were around during that time were very inspiring to me, but Louie was just a genius. A really amazing storyteller. He was always very encouraging to me and a lot of other people who wanted to try comedy but were maybe a little unsure of it at first. To have someone that funny believe in you was a huge boost of confidence."

Others have similar things to say about Anderson, including performers like Stephanie Hodge and Susan Vass. For Anderson, it was less about trying to mentor future comedians and more about paying forward his experience and good fortune. "I think that if you know something, you should share it with somebody else," he says.

Once the divide started to emerge at Mickey Finn's, Anderson realized he needed to step up and look for a new creative outlet. He turned to longtime improv king Dudley Riggs and eventually started a new comedy group at one of Riggs's theater spaces.

Still, he says, stand-up wasn't receiving the respect he believed it deserved in the local arts scene. "People will lump stand-up in with all of comedy, but it's not the same thing," Anderson says. "We were the stepchild of comedy. And we still are. But for me, it is probably the most fun job anybody could have."

Anderson had played an integral role in building the Twin Cities comedy scene, but when two of his most trusted mentors suggested that he make the jump to one of the coasts, he knew it was time to move on. "Rodney [Dangerfield] said I should go to New York, and Joan [Rivers] said I should go to New York or LA," Anderson recalls. "So I decided to go out to LA because I was tired of the cold weather."

After hosting, by his count, "about a hundred" farewell shows in Minnesota to gather enough money, Anderson packed up his 1978 Malibu Classic, shoved $600 in his pocket, and headed west, where an old friend was ready to greet him with open arms.

"Jeff Gerbino had moved out there a little while before, so he let me rent a room from him and his wife in the Valley," Anderson says.

Anderson had made it to Los Angeles, but he had a long way to go before he "made it" as an LA comic. "I got really lucky to get out there and was lucky to know people and get sets," he says. "Eventually, it was Jimmie Walker who got Mitzi Shore, the woman who owned the Comedy Store, to watch my set so that I could become a regular. Then eventually I became a paid regular, and then it became my goal to get my name on the outside of the building, and I did that."

Before getting his name up in lights, however, Anderson nearly fizzled out of the Los Angeles comedy scene altogether. He was broke, and he had applied for a job at a local mini-mart. That same day, he got a call to perform on *The Tonight Show Starring Johnny Carson.* "I called the guy [at the mini-mart] and said, 'I'm not going to

Ad for one of Louie Anderson's farewell gigs before he left the Twin Cities for Hollywood

need the job. I got *The Tonight Show* last night.' He laughed and said, 'Yeah, sure you did.' So I told him to go ahead and watch me, then," Anderson remembers.

One of the details often left out of this now-famous story is that Anderson, a couple of years earlier, had been told by the person in charge of booking comedians that he "wasn't *Tonight Show* material."

It was a stab in the heart for any comedian of that era, but Anderson continued to work at his craft. Then one day, the competition came calling.

"The people who booked *Late Night with David Letterman* had seen me perform somewhere in New York or LA when they were looking for new comics to bring on the show," Anderson recalls. "They saw me and wanted to book me."

In what would be one of Anderson's first uncomfortable lessons in the ways of show business, as soon as he had lined up his first big-time late-night comedy set with Letterman, *The Tonight Show* suddenly expressed interest too. "When the Letterman people wanted me, then the *Tonight Show* people wanted me," he says. "I had a lot of misgivings about doing *The Tonight Show*, but this was my dream come true. I wanted to do *The Tonight Show* with Johnny Carson."

Although he felt guilty, Anderson went through with *The Tonight Show*. "I felt terrible. I felt really bad and regretted it," Anderson says about canceling on Letterman. "But eventually Dave and the producers forgave me, and eventually I was able to do his show too. But the guy who booked me on *The Tonight Show* never wanted me until I was going to do the other show. I think the only reason [he called] was that he felt like he was going to miss out on me. Maybe he didn't like fat people, I don't know."

Misgivings aside, that first *Tonight Show* appearance in November 1984 would change the trajectory of Anderson's career forever. "I remember Johnny laughing really hard," Anderson fondly recalls. "That was what I was listening for. The audience was nice, but you wanted to hear him hit that desk."

After finishing his set, Anderson got the biggest and most important endorsement of his comedy career to that point: Carson brought him back out for a handshake. "That was a really big deal," he says. "I went from making a couple of hundred dollars a week to a few thousand dollars a week basically overnight thanks to that handshake."

Soon, he was touring with Roseanne Barr, who had been a frequent performer in Minneapolis and was on the rise nationally, and he appeared on a national television special performing for President Ronald Reagan. Anderson became a fixture on the late-night talk show circuit, winning over new crowds with his low-key, family-friendly style.

Despite the successes, however, Anderson struggled to find a way to get his comedy out to audiences in a longer, "packaged" special. So he returned to the place where he got his first taste of television stardom. "I couldn't get a special," Anderson says bluntly. "So I came back to Minnesota and reached out to KTCA [the local PBS affiliate]. I said, 'If you guys shoot a special, I'll let you use it as a fundraiser for the station. Then we'll own it together and sell it afterward.'"

The station agreed, and Anderson went on to record *Louie Anderson at the Guthrie* in 1987. The special was renamed *Mom! Louie's Looking at Me Again!* when it was sold to Showtime less than a year later.

"It cost $17,000 to make it; I sold it for $40,000," he recalls. "And it was great because that made a lot of money for PBS."

The reviews were overwhelmingly positive. In a piece about Anderson and the special on the day it first aired on Showtime, *New York Times* television critic John J. O'Connor wrote, "At a time when standup comedy is trafficking heavily in insult, hysteria and sexual obsessions, Mr. Anderson seems to have come up with something truly different—old-fashioned, heartwarming humor."

The prophecy that Roman Dicaire had handed down years prior had come to fruition. Anderson was a star.

"It was the highest-rated comedy special ever on Showtime," Anderson says proudly. "A lot of younger comics have told me that was the special that really encouraged them and made them think they could do stand-up."

After the success of that first special, the sky was the limit for Anderson. Multiple specials on HBO and Showtime would follow, along with TV shows and movie appearances. He was headlining sold-out tours across the country. By the end of the 1980s, Anderson had made a name for himself as one of the most consistently funny comedians around.

Still, more than four decades later and having built a career as one of the most successful stand-up comics in history, Anderson says his formative memories and motivation for getting onstage can be traced back to those nights at Mickey Finn's many decades ago.

"Even when I get onstage now, I just feel alive," he says. "I was twenty-five years old when I started, and I felt so alive and full. There was nothing better than killing a crowd on a Saturday night, even in those little fifty-seat rooms like Mickey Finn's. And then, you know, I'd go out and try to start my car in the fifty-below weather."

··· 6 ···

Alex Cole

In 1979, the *Twin Cities Reader* ran a cover story about the emerging Twin Cities stand-up comedy scene. Jeff Gerbino was featured on the cover of the alt-weekly dressed in a bathrobe and standing triumphantly at the top of a staircase, channeling his best Rocky Balboa. This feature caught Alex Cole by surprise.

"I looked at it like, 'Twin Cities comedy? I *am* Twin Cities comedy. What the hell? I don't know anything about this,'" Cole recalls.

Although his comedy peers, namely cover boy Jeff Gerbino, would mock him for thinking so highly of himself, the truth is that Cole had a pretty legitimate gripe.

Cole got his first taste of comedy in Minneapolis in 1970 at the age of fifteen. "Me and my friends started a Christian sketch improv troupe," he says. "We were called Clyde Digit and Family. We'd perform in church basements all over town. I know it sounds crazy, but it was a great way to learn comedy because we had to be clean and perform to the audience. We actually traveled around and got pretty big in the five-state area."

Soon, Cole wanted to take things to the next level, but the rest of the troupe was interested in staying in their comfortable church circle. So, all of sixteen years old, Cole decided he was ready to make the move to the big time. "I went down to the Brave New Workshop theater and said I wanted to talk to Dudley," he recalls with a laugh. "That shows you how much I understood how things worked. Surprisingly, he agreed to talk to me. We sat down over an espresso, and he asked me how old I was. I told him I was sixteen, and he goes, 'Oh, that's a little young. You need to be at least twenty-one.' But he told me that if I wanted to, I could come by and sweep up on Wednesday nights and he'd let me have a ticket to watch the show. I did that for about six months, and that was my first time meeting Dudley."

Soon after, Cole enrolled in North Hennepin Junior College to focus on his original love: acting. "I made the decision when I was maybe ten years old that I wanted to become an actor," Cole says. "I grew up watching *The Andy Griffith Show*, and I wanted to be Opie. So when I started watching sitcom stars like Jimmie Walker and Freddie Prinze, and I read that they got discovered doing stand-up, I figured I could do that too."

With no real training and no proper stand-up comedy venue, Cole developed his act through trial and error, opening for musical acts performing in the Twin Cities. "It was just about finding any opportunity to get onstage," he says.

One day, Cole came across a flyer on campus informing him that one of his comedy influences was coming to town. "Jimmie 'JJ' Walker was coming to do a nooner, a daytime show, in the student union," Cole recalls. "I went to the show and I got to talk with him after, so I asked, 'How do you get booked to do this?' And he was nice enough to give me a card of the guy who booked it."

Despite the newfound connection, Cole decided to leave town to pursue his acting dreams, heading to New Jersey to join the Hoboken Street Theater. A year later, in 1975, he returned to Minneapolis to join the Acme Theatre Company (no relation to the later Acme Comedy Company), located in the newly opened Riverside Café on Cedar Avenue. "It was a bunch of ex-hippies," he says. "You'd get people playing songs, and then the group I was in would perform sketches."

The following year, Cole and a fellow actor formed their own comedy group, McDonald and Cole, while continuing to pursue traditional acting jobs around town. By this point, having gained more experience as a performer and actor, Cole decided the time had come to revisit Dudley Riggs. "Dudley was so great," he recalls. "I went to him and asked, 'Could I do stand-up after your shows for free?' I doubt he remembered me from years before, but I knew he was a good guy, so I felt like it was worth asking. And he said yes. So on Wednesday nights after the show at the theater, they'd let me do a half hour of stand-up. People really didn't know what the hell it was at that point, but I could make people laugh and was getting pretty good at it."

That's when Cole remembered the meeting with Jimmie Walker. "I still had that card he gave me," he says. "So I called the person who had booked that college show and told him that I'm a comedian. He invited me to his office, and I went and did my act, right there in his office, and he signed me. He told me to come up with another fifteen minutes of material and he'd put me on the college circuit."

Cole was off and running. He was soon performing shows at colleges all over the country, developing his act and making a solid living at the same time. "I had my act, and it was a theater act," he recalls. "I was doing some nooners, but mostly I was just doing concert comedy with real audiences that came specifically to see a show."

When he returned to Minneapolis, he heard about Mickey Finn's and the scene being developed by Jeff Gerbino, Bill Bauer, and Scott Hansen. "Unbeknownst to me, these guys had started a club," he remembers. "I didn't know anything about them, but they were doing a show at the Walker Church, so I decided to go down and introduce myself. They were all nice guys, and they invited me to come down to Mickey Finn's."

Despite the fact that he was a seasoned performer at that point, Cole admits that writing and performing for the club crowd was a much different experience. "Mickey Finn's was interesting. I was used to the audiences that came to my college shows, and now I'm in this union bar where you'd have nights where nobody gave a fucking rat's ass about stand-up comedy," Cole laughs. "But overall, the room was rocking. It was a great place to work. You could try anything."

Having already experienced comedy crowds in some more well-established cities, Cole saw how different it was to perform in Minneapolis. "The audiences were really nice, very polite," he says. "Honestly, the entire renaissance of nightclub comedy in the seventies was so exciting to see live. As performers, we were all still learning how to perform in front of an audience that was still learning how

Alex Cole at Mickey Finn's.
(Courtesy of Alex Cole)

to be a comedy audience. No one had really experienced stand-up comedy except for the little bit they might catch on television, so Mickey Finn's was really the only place to see it live."

Cole continued to perform regularly at Mickey Finn's for a while, but the lure and money of the college circuit ultimately was too much to pass up. "By the time all was said and done, I ended up performing over 1,700 college shows," he says. "Colleges were a great way to make money. But they didn't have the same intimate feel of performing at a comedy club."

As more clubs started opening around the country, Cole was able to book himself in new venues and territories when they coincided with his college tour schedule, broadening his exposure and experience. He was also making connections with these clubs, creating a path for talent swapping between Minneapolis and other cities, further establishing Minneapolis as a "comedy town."

"Word got out that Minneapolis was a cool place to do comedy," he recalls, "so that made it easy for me to book a couple of club shows in places where they were just starting to figure out their own comedy scenes. Kansas City had a room, Denver, Detroit—they all heard about what was happening in Minneapolis and started trading acts

The Students' Choice!
1988 Campus Comedian of the Year!

ALEX COLE

In all your life, you never laughed so hard.

Arne Brav Associates
———— artist representation ————

Alex Cole was named the 1988 campus comedian of the year by the National Association for Campus Activities (NACA), a coveted title for any comic. (Courtesy of Alex Cole) back and forth with Mickey Finn's and eventually other rooms in town."

When the sun finally began to set on Mickey Finn's and the original five pursued other paths, Cole joined up with fellow original Louie Anderson and other comics to launch a new chapter in Twin Cities comedy. The Minneapolis Comedy All-Stars, run out of Dudley Riggs's Experimental Theater Company, allowed Cole to combine his loves of comedy and acting, and it provided a new and innovative venue for live comedy in the Twin Cities.

By the end of the eighties, having cemented his spot as the king of college comedy and as one of the top local comics, Cole was primed to enter the next phase of his career. Or so he thought. "1988 through 1990 were the best years of my career," he recalls. "I signed with ABC

Alex Cole onstage.
(Courtesy of Alex Cole)

for a pilot in '88. Unfortunately, that was when the writer's strike happened. Then I signed a three-year deal with the Desert Inn in Las Vegas to perform eight weeks out of the year. At that point, I thought I had done everything I was supposed to for the next step."

But with a wife and kids at home, Cole stuck with what he knew. "I probably stayed in the colleges longer than I should have, but when you have bills, you do what you have to," he says. "Eventually, by 1990, I started getting pushed out of the college market by Carrot Top. He was cheaper than me, and all the kids thought he was just the greatest thing. So I decided it was time to do something else."

Cole eventually returned to Minnesota to pursue an acting career, and he worked in the vibrant Twin Cities theater scene for roughly a decade. Still, he would take the occasional stand-up gig in order to stay sharp—until one show finally convinced him it was time to hang it up. "I did a Christmas show in Minnetonka at an Italian restaurant," he says. "It was for a law firm, and there were maybe twelve people there. No stage, no lights, and no PA system. And I went out there and kicked their asses. I took the place apart, because that's what I was trained to do. After the show, I sat in my jeep letting it warm up, and thought, 'I didn't sign up to be doing this at fifty fucking years old.' So I called my agents and said, 'Cancel everything. I'm done.'"

Now living in Florida, Cole still performs music but has stayed true to his retirement from comedy. Nevertheless, his influence in terms of both talent and work ethic rubbed off on his comedy peers, and he helped to raise the bar not only in the quality of the performers but also in the audience's expectations.

"The bar got raised for everyone," he says. "There was still plenty of room for the new guys who were trying to find their way, working a day job and then performing at night. But when it came to the guys like myself and Hansen and Louie and everybody, the guys who were making some money and doing this as their profession, the audience knew they could and should expect more from us. They knew if you were just up there babbling some insane bullshit. And as the audiences started to expect more, the acts either got better or they quit."

For Cole, whether he was performing in dingy clubs in front of a handful of disinterested drunks or at colleges in front of hundreds of eager youngsters, his legacy is defined by his hard work, showmanship, and unmatched ability as a performer. "It really wasn't that hard for me," he says nonchalantly. "After maybe three times performing I had forty-five minutes of material. I'm not the funniest guy in the world, but I know how to do the work. I know how to make people laugh. You tell me how many people are in the audience and how long you need me to perform and I can pull that off."

... 7 ...

Scott Hansen

If the legend is to be believed, Scott Hansen was born into comedy. Or rather, he was born because of comedy.

"My mom claims that her water burst one night while she was watching a clown on television called the Banana Man," Hansen deadpans. "He was a character, a mime act, who would come out and pull all these props out of his costume and get surprised by things and make a noise. She was watching and started laughing so hard that she went into labor, and we were off."

Whether that story is true or not, Hansen was a comedy fan from a young age. He used school writing assignments as his first foray into comedy. "I'd try to make them funny, try to make people laugh," he recalls. "It made it easier and more interesting for me."

Like many other future comedians of his generation, Hansen got his first exposure to stand-up watching *The Tonight Show* on television with his father. "He would let me stay up for the comedians," Hansen says. "I loved it. My favorites were always the guys who could make the other comedians laugh. I knew it was something I really wanted to do. Either that or become a priest. Anything where I could perform in front of a crowd."

His desire to try comedy may have been with him early on, but the opportunity to get onstage wasn't. That is, until he met Bill Bauer.

Hansen's first encounter with the future wild man of Twin Cities comedy was through Bill Bauer's brother, Tim, who was a school friend of Hansen's. "One time I was over at his house, and Bill had just returned from Vietnam," Hansen recalls of their first encounter. "Bill bursts into the room and goes, 'I brought an entire gunnysack full of pot back with me, and I'm going to smoke all of it.' To the best of my knowledge, that's exactly what he did."

A few weeks later, Bauer signed up to compete in the comedy contest at Mickey Finn's, and he invited Hansen to come watch the show. That night, a connection was made.

"I didn't perform that night; I just watched the show," Hansen says. "The thing about that show was, when you put up a sign that says 'Comedy Contest,' people come out of the woodwork. Everyone thinks they're funny until they try it. So there were a lot of guys who had never done it before who weren't all that good. But I still couldn't believe there was a show that was all stand-up comedy."

After a few return visits to Mickey Finn's and keeping a low profile in the audience, Hansen finally got up the courage to get onstage himself. "I was scared shitless," he says of his first time performing. "I waited a few weeks because I was so scared to try it. I had a horrible fear of public speaking. I'd practice my jokes at home and try to memorize things because that's how I thought you did it."

He also got in the habit of creating cheat sheets to help prompt him into his next heavily rehearsed joke. "My very first joke would be, 'I'm Scott Hansen, and I come from a mixed marriage. I'm half Lutheran and half Catholic. Are there any Catholics here tonight?'" Hansen remembers. "And some people would clap, and then I'd pull out my little cheat sheet and say, 'Great. Anybody want to buy a raffle ticket?' and then set it on the stool as my crutch."

Hansen would continue practicing the same jokes over and over, performing the exact same set week after week until he found himself becoming more comfortable onstage. Around this time, he approached Jeff Gerbino, who had taken the reins at the Mickey Finn's comedy nights. Hansen made it clear to Gerbino that he was interested in becoming a regular fixture of the comedy scene. "I stopped him in the little hallway where the comics would wait before they went onstage and told him I wanted to keep doing this, and he called me later that week," Hansen explains. "Jeff had a place to do comedy, but he needed comedians and people he could depend on. So together, he and I decided to start calling all the people who had been in the contest to see if we could get them to come back and perform again. It didn't matter if they were any good or not; we just needed to get more guys onstage."

As for his own comedy, Hansen has always been known among his peers as a prolific writer. But his writing didn't translate to the stage right away.

"I was always writing; I had notes everywhere," he says. "Even to this day, I still write almost every single day. Quite honestly, I've probably forgotten more comedy material than most people have ever come up with. But putting it together was much more difficult. I remember another comic saw me perform one night and said, 'With how good your material is, you shouldn't be bombing as often as you are.' The thing I didn't realize yet was that I needed to find the right character that the audience would be comfortable with. You can write the funniest lines in the world, but if the audience doesn't connect with who you are onstage, it doesn't matter. It took me years to find the right character, and I really had to figure out who I was."

Part of finding that character, Hansen explains, meant not relying on the trendy, easy jokes of the day. As a fairly large man, he made the choice to avoid doing the same-old self-deprecating material about his weight—doing "a few only because they were expected of me," he adds. Instead, Hansen wanted to focus on creating a unique experience for the audience. "Every time I performed, I tried to make sure that what people saw onstage is something they could never see on television," he says. "I wanted it to feel like a very personal performance that was just for them. That meant lots of personal jokes and using those jokes as a way of getting information from the audience, then finding ways to wrap that around what I already had prepared. People didn't realize that my ad-libs were probably two-thirds of the way done before I got onstage, and it was just finding the personal connection for that show. Besides that, I never liked doing political jokes, but I really focused on local things that made people feel like I was talking to them directly."

Developing his comedy meant finding more opportunities to perform. At the time, however, there weren't many existing stages

The Twin Cities, long considered a frigid outpost of Nordic solemnity, has recently become a hotbed of humor. Here's a look at some of the area's funniest stand-up comedians, and what it's like to get laughs for a living.

Scott Hansen

It happens every time I get up here—people stare at me. I know what you're thinking: "Boy, is that guy tall."

SCOTT HANSEN *IS* TALL, but, more obviously, he's *big,* "a mountain of a man," as one critic put it. He uses his weight disarmingly in his act, assuming a quiet, modest demeanor that's weirdly out of sync with his proportions.

Hansen, 29, runs the Comedy Gallery, which he started two years ago after a year with the Comedy Cabaret. Often he books national acts at the Gallery, with local comics as openers. Hansen himself performs every weekend, though not always in the Twin Cities—he has done his act in Los Angeles and New York City.

If there had been a degree available in stand-up comedy, Hansen might have stayed

at the University of Minnesota, where he studied theater. Instead, he became a warehouse worker. In 1978, after canceling out twice because of nerves, he went on stage at Mickey Finn's, first making sure that he had 20 good laughers in the audience—his friends and relatives. "It was the scariest feeling I've ever had in my life," he remembers, and it was two years before he overcame that stage fright. He still has anxieties. "Basically I'm nervous that I'm going to forget something, so I've had to develop tricks," he says. "I write things on my hand—see?" Recently he bought a home computer to store his material. "You forget so much," he laments.

Obviously, business is picking up. As a warehouse worker, he sometimes was performing five or more nights a week, while having to be at the warehouse job at 7:00 A.M. His wife, Michele, encouraged him to devote full time to comedy. "I still couldn't make a living at comedy," he says, "but it's getting better." He is trying to create a comedians' clearinghouse, to find work for local comics that will keep them in Minnesota, and he's trying to develop a local comedy show for cable TV.

Hansen even dreams of a national TV appearance. "I've got a file of things for when I get on the *Tonight Show,*" he admits. "One of them might be about the smallest show I ever did." Let's see... that would be back in 1981, the day President Reagan was shot. When Hansen stepped out for an open stage that night, he found only one person in the audience. She had a dollar-off coupon for the 99-cent show. "Why are you out?" he asked. "Don't you read the newspapers?" She explained, "My coupon expires tonight."

Scott Hansen
"I write things on my hand—see?"

Scott Hansen outside of Shinders bookstore and newsstand in Minneapolis, as pictured in Minnesota Monthly magazine, April 1984. (Courtesy of Scott Hansen)

beyond Mickey Finn's, so it was up to Hansen to create those opportunities for himself. "Locally, we were able to get connected with a guy named Bill Warner who owned a few different bars around town," Hansen says. Warner recognized the attention Hansen and other comics were getting over at Mickey Finn's, and he decided to take a chance on Hansen. Warner also recognized that it was cheap entertainment. "He had the Artists' Quarter, Williams Pub, and a place called the Country House, and he was paying us fifty bucks a night to hold shows at all of these clubs."

However, just because the bar was willing to host comedy didn't mean the patrons became comedy fans overnight. "Each club had its own flavor and its own customers," he explains. "The Artists' Quarter, for example, was a biker bar, and the bikers wanted it to be their bar. So a guy coming in to tell jokes and make fun of the bikers didn't always work out."

Still, as comedy gained traction locally and nationally, each club Hansen performed at would help to build an audience, as well as encourage new comedians to test their chops. Despite this expanding market, Hansen still wasn't sure where comedy fit into his long-term goals. "I would have been very happy to make [comedy] a hobby, something I could do for fun," he shares. "My goal long term in my head was to be a television writer or a radio DJ. Around this time, I actually did audition for Brown College to see if I had the diction and the voice to be in radio. I had read that George Carlin, who was always one of my favorites, started his career in radio and then became a comedian. I figured that if I started as a comedian, I could make my way into radio. But then I started to see all the radio DJs in the area were coming out to our shows and trying to be stand-up comics. That's when I realized there was a pecking order, and the way it was, I was above them. So I decided, I'll stick to this."

He decided to pursue his hobby full time. "I'm getting paid like $200 a week, which was big money back then, so I figured, hell, I'm quitting my job."

At the time, Hansen was working as a warehouse manager for a vending company. He had worked for the company since he was fourteen years old, thanks in part to the fact that his father was the company's president. By now Hansen was married to his wife, Michelle, and the couple was expecting their first child. Despite the uncertainty that came with pursuing his artistic passion, in an industry that had yet to be established, he knew deep down comedy was what he wanted to do. He also knew he was fortunate to have an incredible support system. "Michelle gave me all the support I could ask for," he says. "She knew this was what I wanted, and so she said, 'quit, quit, quit!'"

And quit he did, in dramatic fashion. "I was sitting there at four in the morning cleaning floors, and the commissary guy walks right across my freshly mopped floor," he recalls. "So I lost it. I hauled back and smacked him in the face with the mop and decided I was done. I talked to my dad and explained I just couldn't do it anymore, that I was going to do comedy full time and I didn't care."

With the support of his wife, a broken mop handle, and several nights of shows lined up each week, Scott Hansen had made the move to become a full-time comedian. And then, just three weeks later, Bill Warner decided he no longer wanted to have comedy at any of his bars. "A lot of times, we'd come in and do these shows and build an audience," Hansen says, "and all of a sudden the owners would think they don't need comedy anymore. They're not thinking that maybe the comedy was why people were coming in at all."

Eventually, Warner reconsidered and allowed the guys to once again host comedy shows in his bars. But Hansen realized he needed to think bigger if he was going to make a real living in his newfound profession.

"We had started getting calls because of the press we were getting locally," he remembers. "We'd also make calls to the college towns and see if we could get ourselves booked. There was one show we did in Mankato where we were treated like kings. They put us up in a fancy hotel and fed us these amazing dinners. Then the day of the show, the local radio station came to us and said they wanted to broadcast it live. A few months after that, a guy from Northfield who was with National Public Radio came to us and said he wanted to put together some comedy shows that he could broadcast nationally. Pretty soon, people all over were starting to find out about us. It was pretty fun."

As the new decade rolled around, stand-up comedy was catching on nationally. Comedians like Steve Martin and Rodney Dangerfield were breaking big with Grammy-winning live albums, and new comedy clubs were opening across the country. Things continued to grow in the Twin Cities as well, with a new influx of talented performers arriving on the scene. Meanwhile, Hansen and the rest of the original five were beginning to see their own hard work pay off with new opportunities for stage time and a growing fan base. But with tensions growing within the group, capped off by the fight between Hansen and Bauer, things had broken down to the point that Hansen was prepared to walk away for good.

"After the incident with Bill, I got out of there and came home and told my wife that I can't do it anymore," Hansen says. This was around 1980, just before the birth of his first son. "It was getting really, really crowded," he said of the exploding comedy scene at the time. "So I took a year off and tried a couple of different businesses."

Coffee salesman, manager for a seafood warehouse, and even playing Santa Claus door-to-door were all ways he was able to make ends meet. "It was fun, but honestly I was doing anything to raise cash," he says.

Around that same time, Hansen saw an article in the local paper announcing that Mickey Finn's alum Gail Matthius had been tapped to join the cast of *Saturday Night Live*. "I called to congratulate her, and I didn't realize she was living with Scott Novotny, another comedian who had started to steer clear of the drugs and all the bullshit at Mickey Finn's," Hansen recalls. "So we started talking, and I told him we should get a place together. A lot of the comics had been calling and saying they were sick of Mickey Finn's and were looking for a new place to perform."

That conversation planted the seed that would sprout the next phase of the Twin Cities stand-up scene.

8

Welcome to the Comedy Cabaret

As the 1980s began, stand-up comedy was on fire. Nationally, names like George Carlin, Robin Williams, and Steve Martin were becoming regular fixtures on TV. Locally, Mickey Finn's was still pulling in consistently strong crowds, out-of-town comedians were coming to perform for Twin Cities audiences, and even comedy forefather Dudley Riggs was expanding his shows to include stand-up.

While the growth of stand-up comedy was great for fans and provided more opportunities for performers, things were still pretty hectic when it came to getting stage time. "Mickey Finn's was basically just Bill and Alex by then, because Jeff left for Los Angeles in 1980 or '81," recalls Hansen. "At that point, it was just a drug den."

That's not to say that the quality of comedians or the quantity of fans at Mickey Finn's had dipped, but without Hansen or Gerbino to maintain order, things could get a little out of hand. "We called ourselves the Comedic Revolutionary Council," recalls Cole, "and we had handbills made up that we handed out all over Riverplace [in Minneapolis]. At that point we had moved the stage into the basement of Mickey Finn's, and we had people like Lizz Winstead and Sid Youngers working there quite a bit. The difference between how it was with Scott in charge and what it was like with us in charge was that Scott really didn't like pushing envelopes. Billy loved it, and I was always kind of a revolutionary-minded person. So the feeling at Mickey Finn's became, go up there and do whatever you want. Take a shit onstage if you want, as long as it gets a laugh."

"The Comedic Revolutionary Council" took over Mickey Finn's after Jeff Gerbino left for California.

coupon

THE COMEDIC REVOLUTIONARY COUNCIL

Proudly announces
their

Triumphant Return
to

MICKEY FINN'S

Friday
1 show 9 p.m.
Saturday
2 shows 8 & 10:30 p.m.

featuring

BILL BAUER & ALEX COLE

379-3379

312 Central Ave.

2 for 1 Admission
with this ad

The insanity wasn't contained to the stage, either. One night, Bauer managed to procure some horse tranquilizers, and Cole decided to give them a try. As legend has it, he passed out in the Mickey Finn's elevator and missed the entire show. When he finally came to, he demanded that he be paid for the two shows he believed he had already performed that night. Bauer, who had been drinking for size all evening, ended up in a shouting match with his friend, partly over the money, partly because neither of them was really sure what had happened.

While Bauer and Cole were raising hell at their old haunt, some of the comedians who had grown tired of the Mickey Finn's scene or were interested in finding more stage time reached out to Hansen. Hansen had been in touch with Scott Novotny, a Dudley Riggs alum who was looking for his next move after his comedy partner, Gail Matthius, left town to join *Saturday Night Live*. Hansen and Novotny were exploring starting something new together.

Novotny's journey in comedy was different from Hansen's. He and Matthius had performed at the Mickey Finn's stand-up shows, but they were interested in engaging in a wider variety of comedy beyond stand-up. "Gail and I were friends from our college days, and we decided to start a comedy group called Amalgamated Amusement Company," Novotny says. "We picked the name so we could be AA Company in the Yellow Pages, when people still cared about those."

Soon after, he joined Dudley Riggs, where he spent three years as part of the resident troupe. By the early 1980s, Novotny knew he was ready to move on to something new. That's when he and Hansen decided to join forces and open their own club.

With Hansen taking the role of business manager and Novotny acting as artistic director, a partnership was formed. In February 1981, the Comedy Cabaret opened its doors and became the first stand-alone comedy club in Minnesota.

Located at Twenty-Eighth Street and Hennepin Avenue in the Uptown neighborhood of Minneapolis, the 120-seat theater was far more of a performance space than most of the other makeshift stages Hansen had helped champion around town. Still, Hansen and Novotny employed the same do-it-yourself mentality that helped to shape Mickey Finn's a few years earlier. "We got the seats out of an old synagogue in St. Paul," Hansen recalls. "They were nailed down to the floorboards, so we had to pull them up and move them over to our place."

The building was located across the street from an elementary school, which made it impossible for the club to get a liquor license. What some might have considered a deterrent would actually be a benefit to the Cabaret. They sold coffee, water, soda, and candy, but without the pressures of making their money from alcohol, Hansen and Novotny were able to focus on the comedy. "Not having alcohol really helped us because it brought us a lot of younger performers and

Minneapolis Tribune   Sun., Feb. 22, 1981   11G

Comedy Cabaret to feature variety entertainment

Maybe vaudeville isn't dead, only lurking in dark places ready to spring out and grab you. At any rate, the latest effort to revive variety entertainment, The Comedy Cabaret, will open its doors at 1414 W. 28th St. Friday and Saturday for shows both nights at 8 and 10:45. The brains behind the effort are artistic director Scott Novotne, a Dudley Riggs Brave New Workshop grad, and managing director Scott Hansen, a stand-up comic. Setting up the cabaret, above, are The Comedy Cabaret Players, from left, Ed Noreen, Hansen, Novotne and Ronnie Douglas. The opening weekend features them plus comedian Jeff Gerbino, some singers, a magician and more. After the opening, the cabaret will go to a weekly schedule, Monday through Thursday at 8 p.m. with the featured revue on weekends. Mondays will be an open stage. Tuesdays will include magic acts and cabaret singers. Wednesday is billed as "Anything Goes," which could include hypnotists, puppet shows, barbershop quartets or all together. Thursday is devoted to stand-up comedy. An open-stage jazz concert follows each show.

On February 22, 1981, the Minneapolis Tribune *ran a piece about the opening of the Comedy Cabaret: (from left) Ed Noreen, Scott Hansen, Scott Novotny, and Ron Douglas.*

audiences who knew they wanted to see comedy, but they didn't want to deal with the bar scene that went with it to that point," Hansen recalls.

They chose the name Comedy Cabaret to reflect the variety of entertainment that Novotny hoped to bring into the space. "Scott wanted to focus on stand-up, and he was able to bring in a lot of really good comedians," Novotny says. "For me, I wanted to do the stand-up stuff but also make it more of a variety show. I was a lot more appreciative of all forms of entertainment. My vision was that we'd have everything from mimes to a cappella groups. I really wanted to bring back the era of vaudeville. I wanted people to know that when they came down to the Cabaret, they could see anything."

The club's opening weekend featured stand-up performances from Hansen and Novotny, as well as fellow comedians Ed Noreen and Ron Douglas, and a special performance by Hansen's old partner, Jeff Gerbino. They also had singers and hypnotists and puppet shows, and they opened the doors to other types of performers who would eventually try their hands at stand-up.

One of those performers was Peter Staloch, who had just moved to Minneapolis in 1981 after graduating with a theater degree from St. John's University. Having worked with Novotny as an actor in the past, Staloch was intrigued when he found out what the Comedy Cabaret had to offer. "I called him [Novotny], and he said come on down and do some improv classes with him," Staloch recalls. "So I went and met Scott Hansen, who was coordinating the stand-up portion of the theater, and the tech director, Don Fitzwater, who had just left Dudley Riggs's Brave New Workshop, and Cliff Walentsky, who was the musical director. Novotny said that his goal was to create a more variety-flavored venue to compete with Dudley Riggs, and he was interested in creating a sketch and improv troupe for the club. So I joined because I was more interested in sketch, improv, and satire. Stephanie Hodge was another actor who was interested in performing as well. The three of us, along with actor Phil O'Donnell, became the Comedy Cabaret Players."

The group put on its first revue in August 1981. Entitled "The All Generic Revue, Featuring Sketches 1–15," the show was well received by fans and critics, and the Comedy Cabaret was firing on all cylinders. "Things went really well," Hansen says. "We were getting some really good comics coming in all of a sudden. One of those was a guy named Joel Hodgson."

Hodgson, who is best known today as the mastermind behind the

Phil O'Donnell is the Dad, Stephanie Hodge is the Mom, Scott Novotone is the Son and Peter Staloch is the Swede (the Plant plays itself) in the "All Generic Revue Featuring Sketches 1 through 15" at 8 and 10:30 p.m. today and Saturday in the Comedy Cabaret, 1414 W. 28th St.

The Comedy Cabaret's "All Generic Revue, Featuring Sketches 1–15" players: (from left) Scott Novotny, Phil O'Donnell, Peter Staloch, and Stephanie Hodge. (From the Minneapolis Tribune)

iconic *Mystery Science Theater 3000*, started his performing career in the seventh grade as a magician and ventriloquist. He attended Bethel University, studying theater and mass media. Hodgson continued to develop his magic act in college, and he began to incorporate comedy into his routine. After opening for musicians on campus and trying his act at coffee shop open mics, Hodgson knew the Comedy Cabaret was the platform he had been looking for to get his act in front of larger audiences.

With his punk rock haircut and white tailcoat, Hodgson looked like a poor man's Vegas magician. But that look, combined with his sarcastic, disinterested approach to performing tricks, made him one of the first breakout stars of the Cabaret. *Minneapolis Tribune* writer

Mike Steele visited the club about six months into its existence, and he wrote a review that spotlighted Hodgson as a must-see act on the rise. "I don't know where Hodgson can take this act, possibly into something more zany, more magical and more daring, but he is genuinely funny," Steele wrote.

Around this same time, another individual became a major part of the Comedy Cabaret: Novotny's wife, Stephanie Hodge. Hodge had been a barista at Dudley Riggs's Brave New Workshop years prior, and she took classes there. As she found herself more enamored with comedy, she made her way over to Mickey Finn's. "There was nowhere for women to work at all," she recalls. "So I went down to Mickey Finn's and met Louie [Anderson] and Bill Bauer. They were both really good to me. Especially Bill. He was the one guy who told me that it doesn't matter if you're a man or a woman; you just have to be funny. He walked me in, stood by the stage while I performed, and then walked me out again. He was like a big brother."

Hodge and Novotny met at Dudley Riggs and ultimately got married. Hodge continued to perform at Mickey Finn's as well as at Dudley Riggs, but the scene wasn't always welcoming for a female comedian. "It was fine. I was a prop comic at the time. The guys at Mickey Finn's were nice, but they were condescending to me because I was a little girl," she says. "There was a lot of sexism in comedy back then. There still is. But Wild Bill told me one time, 'You know, honey, sometimes you just have to keep talking. Just pretend they like you, or at least notice you, and eventually they will.'"

Hodge echoes what Hansen and Novotny said about the motivation for starting the club, specifically the need for a more comedy-focused venue as an alternative to the typical bar scene. "It was rough at Finn's. It was dark, and people didn't go there for the comedy. It was a bar that was busy being a bar, and that meant lots of booze. When we opened up the Comedy Cabaret, it was more people-oriented. It was well lit, and clearly a club first that had no distractions. Plus, you could see anything there. We had a guy lying on the floor drawing pictures with his toes. We had brand-new baby-faced drag queens. There were jugglers, musicians, magicians. It was more of a comedy carnival than anything else."

While that part of the story holds consistent with others' recollections, Hodge says that it was her and Novotny's idea to start a club, not Hansen's. "I have never been clear on Scott Hansen's role," she says with a laugh. "I didn't know then, and I don't know now. I just know he thought he was supposed to be equal with Scott [Novotny] and me as a third partner."

Hansen is quick to refute Hodge's claim. "After we'd been open a while, [Hodge], who had wanted nothing to do with this club, suddenly decides she wants to be a part of it," Hansen says. "The problem was they didn't realize our partnership wasn't an even split, where they could be two against one. It was 25/25/50."

Despite the uneasy partnership, the Comedy Cabaret flourished. "The audience was there," Novotny recalls. "The appetite for comedy had been brewing."

Adds Hodge, "I sold the tickets, so I got to talk to people who wanted to come in, and a lot of times they had no idea what to expect. Sometimes they'd have trepidation and questions about what it was going to be like, but they heard it was a lot of fun and wanted to see it. Then you had others who had been to Mickey Finn's, and they came in like, 'whoa, fancy!' And others who kind of threw down the gauntlet, like they knew what a comedy show was 'supposed' to be like. But no matter what, people were never unhappy when they got there."

As the club gained momentum, the quality and variety of acts continued to grow. In addition to Hansen and Novotny, and comics like Hodgson who had come over and begun to carve out a niche, others soon followed suit. "We'd get Dudley Riggs performers who wanted to try things," Hodge recalls. "They would do sketches and try things that were a little edgier. And of course we had a lot of people who wanted to try stand-up."

"Everyone was just trying to come up with five or ten minutes of material," says Novotny. "It had a very collaborative feel. It was very underground, and not very commercial. It just felt like something special."

While stand-up was still on the upswing, the Cabaret played host to plenty of other performers who incorporated props and gimmicks into their acts. "I met Penn & Teller at the Renaissance Festival,"

Novotny recalls. "At the time, they were called the Asparagus Valley Cultural Society. They did comedy, but they also incorporated magic. I had the comedy duo Puke & Snot, who were a really popular comedy act at the festival, and I asked Penn & Teller if they wanted to come open for them and work on their act."

Booking Penn & Teller led to Novotny getting connected to another star in the making. "We were the first people outside of Los Angeles to bring in Pee-wee Herman," he says. "I got his number from Penn & Teller, and I called and invited him to come and perform. He said, 'You want me to do a solo show? I only have like fifteen minutes of material.' But he was just so funny that we told him to come out and we'd build a show around that. He had no idea that anyone knew him outside of LA, but we sold out every show. It was really fun to be able to springboard his career."

Another performer who got his start at the Cabaret was Paul Dillery. While Dillery had seen stand-up at Mickey Finn's, he was interested in a different style of comedy and found that the Comedy Cabaret and its theatrical approach was more his speed. "I didn't want to do stand-up," he says casually. "I liked the idea of the Cabaret because they were much more interested in a variety show approach to comedy. I didn't want to talk at all. I wanted to do an act where I didn't talk and just used props and things. And I did for probably the first six months. I never spoke. I had a mandolin that would fly apart and things like that. But I really liked that room because it had a curtain that you came out of, it was very theatrical, and there was no liquor. So I signed up for the open stage on a Monday night, and it went pretty good. I kept coming back, and eventually I decided I wanted to write jokes and talk. I was bringing up a ukulele onstage at the time, and I'd play it, then tell a joke, and then play again while I figured out what to say next."

Other acts came through that were more traditionally stand-up oriented, including Bruce Murray and Chris Raine. Another up-and-coming comedian who showed up at the Cabaret would become a fixture of the Twin Cities comedy scene and have a hand in helping numerous comics find stardom out west later in their careers.

"Stephanie and I met Tom Arnold when we were all doing a show together in Iowa City," Novotny recalls. "He was local and opened for us. After the show, we were all talking, and he said he was planning to go out to LA. We told him he should consider coming to Minneapolis first to work on his act before he headed out there."

Sure enough, Arnold took the couple up on the invite and showed up on their doorstep one night, complete with a horribly ugly shirt, a briefcase full of props, and a bag of goldfish. Soon, the Comedy Cabaret became home to Arnold's "World Famous Goldfish Review." The show featured Arnold playing music while tossing goldfish with the gusto of a Vegas showroom act.

"We put him onstage," Hodge recalls. "He would bring up this badminton racquet with the net cut out, and I'd hold it for him. Then he'd just kind of toss the goldfish through the hoops and say they were jumping. It was dumb, but everybody had a gimmick back then."

Although the Cabaret was open to pretty much anything performers wanted to try, there were a few times performers pushed the boundaries a little too far. "One guy brought his dog onstage, fed it yogurt, it vomited, and he took a bow," recalls Hodge. "I told him, 'You're never allowed to come back here again, and you're cleaning up the vomit.'"

Dillery recalls another performer who pushed the "anything goes" envelope. "There was a guy who would come onstage with a lunch box and two pieces of white bread," he recalls. "And then he'd open the lunch box, and he'd have a live rat inside. He'd say he was making a rat sandwich, and he'd put the rat between the bread, pour barbecue sauce on it, and put it in his mouth. Meanwhile the audience would just be screaming. I didn't really care for that. It was kind of just shock value instead of funny. It was a little like Tom Arnold's goldfish act, but Tom's was actually funny. I don't think the rat comic made it very long."

The club continued to build momentum, but the tensions between Hansen and Hodge would soon boil over. As Hansen tells it, "Stephanie and Scott were doing presentations in schools and corporate gigs Monday through Friday, which left me to run the club. Which was fine, but then they'd show up and decide they knew better."

The first time they butted heads was not long after the club opened. It was the day Ronald Reagan was shot, in March 1981. "I walk in and Stephanie is setting the lineup," Hansen says. "And we've got one person in the audience. So I tell her, 'Stephanie, we're not doing the show.' She says, 'Scott, I come from a theater background, and the show must go on.' So I agreed, but said that I was going to emcee."

Hansen walked out onstage and stared into the eyes of the lone audience member. "I looked at her and said, 'Did you hear what happened today? President Reagan was shot, and they aren't sure if he's going to live.' The woman looks at me, completely terrified, and goes, 'But my coupon expires today.'"

That line got the biggest laugh of the night, from Hansen himself. He offered to refund the woman her two-dollar admission and give her a new coupon for a future show. She accepted and scurried out. Hodge was livid.

"She came out just fuming," Hansen says. "And I had to tell her, 'There is not a comic here who wants to perform for one person.' It was over pretty quickly, but that was the first time we locked horns."

It wouldn't be the last.

Although Novotny had been the one tasked with bringing talent into the club, Hansen says the couple's day jobs took precedence in their lives, leaving him to manage the lineup. "We ran a show called 'Four Comics for Four Dollars,'" Hansen recalls. "It was me, Joel Hodgson, Dan Bradley, and Gary Johnson. We sold out every one of our shows for two weeks straight, and Scott and Stephanie never stepped foot in the building during that time. But when he found out, Novotny was totally pissed that we were running these shows and he wasn't involved."

According to Paul Dillery, that show was a turning point for the club. "The variety-type shows weren't really getting very big audiences," Dillery recalls. "But when they did the 'Four for Four Dollars' show, there were people lined up down the block. I think that was when they really moved toward pretty much all stand-up. It was clear that's what people were coming to see."

Then one night, according to Hansen, his partners pushed him and his fellow performers too far. "I made the lineup for one Friday night, and I made it the week before," Hansen says. "So it's almost

7 PM, which was showtime, and Scott and Stephanie are nowhere to be seen. Then they walk in, five minutes before the show, and cross off everyone's names. In their place, they wrote: First act: Scott Novotny. Second act: Stephanie Hodge. Third act: Novotny and Hodge. I'm sitting there with my mouth hanging open, and Stephanie just says to me, 'We own this club, Scott. We can do whatever we want.' It was really disappointing to me, because I thought we could build something really great, but they were more interested in promoting themselves at that point."

Hodge vehemently denies Hansen's recollection of that night. "He's lying," she says with a laugh. "That never happened. He's full of shit. If we ever did do a show where it was him [Novotny], me, and then the two of us, it was to work out a tour that we were going on. A lot of comics did that. If you're going on tour? Go up on your own, then go up with your partner. But as far as walking in and saying, 'fuck you' like that—it never happened."

While Hansen claims egos were to blame for the rising tensions, Hodge claims money and competition between performers were the real culprits. "They got angry. As soon as we could afford to start paying people, things got more intense," Hodge says. "We'd be having arguments about who deserves to get paid and who doesn't, why certain people aren't being paid but others are. Just a lot of stuff like that. And people started sabotaging each other and talking behind each other's backs. It was a little bit of a daycare center."

Despite Hansen's claims, Hodge insists that providing opportunities for equal stage time were her and Novotny's main priority. "We were there for everybody," she says. "We explained that not one person, including us, deserves more stage time than anyone else in town. But not everyone agreed with that. I remember I would go to Scott and Scott and fight for certain comics to get stage time, especially women and people who I could identify with. But with those two, if the comedian wasn't a certain type of guy, they weren't given stage time. There were women in Minneapolis during that period who were very funny, for example, who deserved stage time and didn't get it. Some of those women held grudges against me, but it wasn't my choice. I spoke up for them, but ultimately it was Scott and Scott who decided."

It was obvious to everybody that all was not well inside the Comedy Cabaret. "As time went by," says Peter Staloch, "it became clear that there were disagreements between the powers that be at the Comedy Cabaret—disagreements over time and show slots, and who gets what, when, and how."

After about a year of tension and arguing, a group of regular performers at the Cabaret asked to have a private meeting with Hansen. It was Joel Hodgson, Peter Staloch and Lee Schmidt (who had formed a comedy duo after Staloch's Comedy Cabaret Players fizzled out), and about four others. Hansen explains, "They came to me and asked, 'What can we do?' At that point, I told them I'd start looking for another spot. However, I decided to talk with Scott and explain how the comics were unhappy, thinking he would understand and change his thinking. All he said to me was, 'Well, just fire them, then. Let them go to Mickey Finn's.'"

Hansen knew the time had arrived for him to get out, but he wasn't sure of his next move. Then one day, the next move found him. "I was at the club one afternoon, and this guy comes in and asks me if I'd be willing to do a print job for him for a restaurant called J. R.'s. I'd been doing some jobs like that on the side just to make extra money, so I told him sure. He comes back a few days later to pick it up, and he says, 'You know you have to get out of here, Scott. Those two [Novotny and Hodge] are hated by the whole entertainment industry.' They had left Dudley with no notice, so they pissed people off there, and then all the stuff that was happening at the club. Novotny had been a great guy, but that woman was just tearing him apart. She had taken over his life."

On the other side of the conversation, Hodge says it wasn't other comedians who had the problem with her, but Hansen himself. "Scott Hansen didn't like me because I didn't keep my place," she says. "I questioned the things he was doing. My money was in this club, so I wanted to know why certain things were happening. When you're a partner, you don't get shut down just because you're some little girl.

But he was very much, 'Don't question me!' before the split. I honestly think he didn't respect me because I was a woman, and because he didn't feel I had earned my spot."

With a comedy divorce clearly on the horizon, Hansen went by J. R.'s Restaurant and Lounge to get a look at the space and scout it as a potential spot for comedy. "I thought it was great," Hansen says. "So I brought some of the comedians over to take a look, and they all agreed that we should start doing comedy there."

Staloch recalls the move from the Cabaret to the new venue: "Along with Joel Hodgson and Don Fitzwater, we told Scott and Stephanie that we were going to move on and start another club. As I recall, they weren't happy about it, but it seemed we were leaving on somewhat friendly terms. Besides, starting another club downtown wouldn't directly compete with the Cabaret, and the fact of another venue would only open new time slots and opportunities for comedians to perform."

Some of the comics were privy to the details of the split, but others, like Dillery, didn't learn of any issues between the owners until they were called to the club one day for a meeting. "I was so innocent," Dillery says. "They said there was a meeting Tuesday night at 7 PM. I showed up a few minutes late, and you could cut the tension in the room with a knife. Scott [Hansen] was up onstage with a few of the comics who were leaving to go to the new club, and Scott [Novotny] and Stephanie were on the other side of the stage with some of the comics who were going to stay with them. The rest of us are in the audience, and they told us Scott was moving to another club."

Although Staloch may have seen the split as amicable, for the former business partners, the competition between the clubs only intensified. "Hansen split and started his own clubs and started telling comedians that if they played his club they couldn't play ours," Hodge says flatly. "It was his loss. We tried to make our stage available for anyone who wanted it. We didn't care where anyone played. No one owned the comics. The way I looked at it, without the comics it was an empty room. So who cares if they played his place two weeks ago? The whole thing was silly and ridiculous. I never understood why he would do that."

Dillery doesn't recall a black-and-white directive about where you could or couldn't perform, but he believes it was something of an unspoken rule. "For a while you couldn't do both," Dillery says. "Nobody actually said it, but it was just sort of known you weren't supposed to do both places. I stayed with Scott and Stephanie because I really liked that room and really didn't think this split affected me very much."

Hansen acknowledges that he was competitive, but he insists it was business, not personal, as to why he went that direction. "They [Novotny and Hodge] were having people as headliners who I didn't believe were at a level where they should be headlining. So I said, 'If you're a headliner at that club, you're a middle act at mine.' Why would anyone want to pay to see someone at my club who had just performed down the street a couple of weeks ago? It was about delivering the best show and the most unique show I possibly could."

Beyond the professional competition, things got ugly between the former partners on the legal front too. "They tried to sue me," Hansen says bluntly when asked about how his defection impacted his relationship with Novotny and Hodge. "We had taken out a loan from Roman Dicaire for $10,000 to get the [Comedy Cabaret] open. I paid off my part, but they tried to tell me I was responsible for the whole thing since I left without notice. I told them to go ahead and show me where that was in our contract, and they couldn't, so that ended that real fast."

The Comedy Cabaret continued on without Hansen for a few more years, until Novotny and Hodge decided to try their luck as performers out in California. "We wanted to see how far we could go, so we sold the club," Hodge says.

The Comedy Cabaret got new owners and became the HaHa Club, and Hodge and Novotny departed for Hollywood. "Before we left town," Novotny adds, "we headlined together and took the profits from the door, which is something we hadn't done to that point, and made a really good little nest egg for us."

Novotny had some success in California, but it was Hodge who became the breakout star. She was featured on an HBO special, *On Location: Women of the Night*, in 1987, alongside rising comics including

Ellen DeGeneres, Paula Poundstone, Rita Rudner, Judy Tenuta, and fellow Minnesotan Lizz Winstead. This led to high-profile acting jobs, starting with a movie role connected to a familiar face from her past. Pee-wee Herman, who had become a megastar by this point, cast Hodge to play the role of a mermaid in the film *Big Top Pee-wee*. Despite their differences, Hodge says she even tried to get Hansen a part, which he refused. "They needed a fat guy, and I thought Scott would be great," she recalls. "I recommended him, and they called him up for the part, but he wanted nothing to do with it."

With her star on the rise, Hodge transitioned to several high-profile TV roles, including on *Nurses* and a starring role in the hit *Unhappily Ever After*. Her marriage to Novotny, however, was not long for Hollywood. "We got divorced almost immediately," she says. "That's when things started to really take off for me, and he and I never really spoke again."

As for the legacy of the Comedy Cabaret, Hodge refuses to take credit for the evolution of the Twin Cities comedy scene. "It disgusts me when people say, 'I'm responsible for so-and-so' or 'Our space is why they were a success.' We were in the right place at the right time and provided a lot of people with the right opportunities. But every comic who became successful deserves the credit. Everyone is responsible for their own well-being."

Novotny, on the other hand, looks back at the Cabaret and remembers a time when comedy was still uncharted territory, and he believes the club helped develop the next phase. "When we started, we didn't have a format. We just needed to know who was available to perform the next weekend and get them booked. We were all working for free, but it was fun," he says. "When Scott left, he started really pushing the three-act format, with an emcee, a feature act, and a headliner, and we were still just kind of going with whatever we thought of for a given night. I don't think there was one right way to do anything. There's a spectrum of what makes things funny and interesting, and the Comedy Cabaret allowed us to explore a lot of it."

··· 9 ···

Dudley Riggs Presents:
The Minneapolis Comedy All-Stars

In the spring of 1981, as the Comedy Cabaret was picking up steam, Mickey Finn's was still a viable option for stand-up comedy. With Bill Bauer at the helm, there were a handful of comedians who stepped in where the original five left off, including Gary Johnson, Dan Bradley, and Chris Raine. In addition, the club was getting a steady stream of new comedy hopefuls looking to get stage time. While this enthusiasm helped to keep the scene growing and comedy fans packing the club, for established names like Louie Anderson, it became a problem.

On any given night, there would be fifteen to twenty comedians seeking stage time at Mickey Finn's. The heavy presence of drugs and alcohol at the club was a further turnoff for Anderson. He realized that in order to continue his own growth as a comedian he would have to pursue other opportunities. He needed to find a venue that was set up for comedy, that had name recognition, and that would allow him to brighten the spotlight on his own career.

He needed Dudley Riggs.

By the early eighties, Riggs had his main theater in downtown Minneapolis and a second space, the Experimental Theater Company (ETC), in an area known as Seven Corners, closer to the University of Minnesota. This second theater space was used primarily by the touring company when they were in town between trips, but most nights it stayed dormant. Anderson had an idea.

"A bunch of us comics were all out there doing our own fifteen minutes and not getting much further," Anderson explains. "We needed a bigger venue; we needed more prestige. Dudley Riggs had more prestige, so I figured I'd go there and see if he could help."

Anderson's name had become well known enough in town that having a conversation with the godfather of improv wouldn't be a fool's errand. So he sat down with Riggs and pitched a one-off idea: a stand-up show with four quality comedians, hand-selected by Anderson. Riggs, who prided himself on presenting shows with a certain standard of quality and creativity, couldn't deny that stand-up comedy was booming and the audience appetite was there. He agreed to a trial run, and Anderson had his stage.

Now he needed comics to fill out the rest of the bill. He set out to put together a lineup that would make an impact and convince Riggs to keep the showcase going. While Anderson himself was becoming quite an attraction locally, he knew he needed another comedian with enough name recognition to make the show stand out from every other open mic or showcase in town. That person was his old friend, Alex Cole.

By this time, Cole had established himself as the biggest comic in town, opening shows at Minneapolis's Orchestra Hall and for rock bands and national comedians when they came through town. In addition to being a solid performer, Cole was very familiar to the media. His name carried credibility and gave the show a big-event "feel." Anderson reached out to Cole, presented some numbers, and soon he had his second man.

"Right around the time that Scott [Hansen] went and started his own club with Scott Novotny, Louie and I are talking about how we should quit trying to fight each other to fill up little bars all over Minneapolis, and to team up," Cole says. "For me it made sense because I was trying to be an actor, and I thought that doing the show would get me noticed faster. That's what everyone was doing at that point. They'd do stand-up and then get a sitcom."

Anderson still needed two more comedians for his showcase. He wanted comics who could open the show but still carry their weight when it came to providing a Dudley Riggs–worthy performance. They needed to be strong performers, reliable, and, above all else, funny.

Joel Madison and Jeff Cesario were two guys who didn't find their way to the stage through chance or curiosity. They came to Minnesota to make names for themselves.

"I was living in San Diego in 1980 and decided to start doing some stand-up," Madison says. "I came back to Minnesota on vacation to see my mom and saw this ad for a comedy night at Mickey Finn's. I went down there and met Bill Bauer and Louie Anderson and Jeff Gerbino. I told them I had been performing some stand-up out in California. They asked if I wanted to go up, and by that time I had probably been doing it for six or seven months, so I had a pretty solid five minutes. I went up and did pretty well, and Louie told me if I ever wanted to get stage time that I could come back."

After returning to San Diego, Madison couldn't shake the feeling that the comedy scene in Minnesota was growing and developing in a way that would give him more opportunity to perform than he could find in California. He packed up and headed back to the Midwest, excited to rejoin the gang and cut his teeth in his new comedy hometown.

Unfortunately, by the time he got back to Minneapolis, the cracks among the original five were beginning to show. "I get back, and Mickey Finn's had fallen apart," Madison says with a laugh. "It was in the middle of whatever war was going on between Scott and Bill and those guys. So I found myself sitting there, new in town, thinking, 'Well, shit. Now what?'"

But just because Mickey Finn's was in disarray didn't mean the comedy scene had dried up, and Madison quickly reconnected with Anderson. "About a month after I got back to town, I saw an ad for a variety club on the university campus," he recalls. "Louie was performing, so I started hanging around and seeing if I could get myself stage time."

Like Madison, Cesario was working to build a career as a performer in the early 1980s when he stumbled upon the burgeoning scene in the Twin Cities. A musician from Wisconsin, Cesario had been hopping around the Midwest, performing in places like Madison, Minneapolis, and Chicago. Then he found his way to Minneapolis the same way many great comics and entertainers did: by following a woman. "I had a girlfriend who moved to Minneapolis in 1980, and back then that was a good enough reason for me to move," Cesario laughs.

While he had some comic chops, Cesario had not really given stand-up a try. "At the time, Mickey Finn's was really the only club in town, and there were maybe fifteen comedians who could do a solid five minutes."

Cesario decided to give it a shot, and similar to Madison's experience, Anderson encouraged him to keep coming back and working on his act. "There was no money in it, but within a year I was doing between two and two and a half hours of stage time each week, which is fucking crazy for how long I had been performing. Honestly, being able to make that many mistakes early on was a godsend for me."

Then one night, Cesario saw Madison when he was performing at Mickey Finn's as part of a two-man comedy team, Lincoln and Madison. "[Lincoln] was much more interested in the duo act than I was," Madison recalls. "I wanted to work on my solo stuff. But when I moved out to Minneapolis, I told him I'd split my time fifty-fifty in terms of working on my own stuff and working with him."

In retrospect, Madison cringes thinking about his early comedy work, but Cesario was impressed with what he saw, and the two became fast friends. "We were the new blood who were just learning rapidly from the guys who started it all," Cesario says.

In addition to their talent as writers and performers, Anderson was also drawn to Madison and Cesario because of their ambition and their lack of baggage. "We came in from out of town and didn't have any agendas or legacy problems," Madison recalls. "We weren't part of the political scene."

Anderson was able to talk the guys into doing the lighting and tech for the show at ETC, as well as providing free labor to promote the event. "Louie handled all the PR, but we'd be the ones who were running around picking up flyers and stuff for him," laughs Cesario.

With the lineup complete, all the group needed was a name. They settled on the Minneapolis Comedy All-Stars. "As soon as we started advertising with that name, everybody else in town got pissed," Cesario says. "They're sitting there thinking, 'Who the fuck do you think you are to call yourselves the All-Stars?' But Louie just blew it off. We were focused on making real money and working on our acts. Plus, I think he liked it because he knew it would piss off Scott and Scott across town."

Anderson says his motivations for choosing the name were much less nefarious. "I felt like anybody could be an all-star," he says, "and we could rotate that with whoever was there at the time. The thing with naming it, and I think Dudley gets most of the credit for this, was that it was kind of like dressing up a pig, in a sense. Except, we were really good. What it did was put a name and a face to comedy, instead of just being a bunch of comedians."

Riggs and Anderson made a deal for a trial run at the theater, but

The Minneapolis Comedy All-Stars: (clockwise from top left) Louie Anderson, Joel Madison, Alex Cole, and Jeff Cesario. (Courtesy of Joel Madison)

Riggs insisted on adding his own vaudeville flair to the show. "Dudley wanted there to be an element that was very Dudley Riggs," Madison recalls. "So he added a magician. The Great Scott, I believe was his name. I remember him because he had a bird act and accidentally tossed a dead dove into the crowd, and it landed right on a table."

Theatrics aside, Anderson had the opportunity he was looking for, and he intended to make the most of it. He told Riggs he didn't need to pay the group, but they would work for the profits from ticket sales. Then, Anderson went to work.

"Louie just knew the business side instinctively," Cesario says. "He was just brilliant. He worked the press relentlessly—and not just trying to get interviews, either. He'd go and talk the shit out of them. He'd play the media off each other. He'd go over to one station and tell them about the show, but then he'd add, 'We just did a really great interview at another paper across town. You probably don't want to cover the same story.' And they would get competitive because they didn't want to miss out on something."

Anderson also connected with a young up-and-coming morning radio host in Minneapolis, Tom Barnard, who had a love of comedy and took a liking to Anderson. Barnard helped to create a local buzz that the Minneapolis Comedy All-Stars were going to be the hottest ticket in town.

With all the pieces in place, the big show finally arrived. To say it delivered would be an understatement.

"We did our first show, and the line was wrapped around the theater," Madison recalls. "Louie had the biggest grin on his face. He had made a huge gamble. There very well could have been eight people there that night. This was long before social media and all of that, so you had no idea what the buzz was like before you showed up."

Adds Cesario, "Louie was giggling [first] because people were there, and second because he had made this insane deal for the door. Dudley would have probably paid us a few hundred bucks together, and instead we ended up making probably a few hundred bucks each. That was big money back then."

The success of that first show helped to solidify their claims of being the hottest ticket in town. After a few more one-off shows, Riggs agreed to make the All-Stars an unofficial comedy Dudley Riggs troupe.

"He gave us like an eight- to ten-week run," Madison says. "It was two acts with an intermission. Me and Jeff would open each half, and Louie and Alex would switch off as to who would close each night. Dudley liked the intermission because it gave the show more of a sense of theater. Stand-up was still so new, and this was really his first time doing it in his clubs. Plus, it gave him a chance to sell more food and booze. Louie agreed to it, no problem. He didn't care. He had the space he wanted and figured he could make it work."

Before long, the Minneapolis Comedy All-Stars were selling out on a regular basis. "We'd sell out every single show," recalls Cole. "Three hundred seats a night. We were rocking. I remember one night, I was living in Coon Rapids at the time in an apartment with my wife and kids, and we're watching Bud Kraehling, the weather guy for WCCO. He's talking about how snowy it's going to be, and how people shouldn't go out. And I'm thinking, 'Shut the fuck up. I got a show to do tonight.' I started driving, and it's slippery and snowy, and I'm thinking, 'This is going to be rough.' When I pulled up to Seven Corners, people were lined up around the building. That's when I knew we were kicking some serious ass."

As the shows continued to draw massive crowds, the All-Stars became an even hotter ticket than the Dudley Riggs players. "Suddenly we had the touring company pissed off at us too," Madison adds. "Dudley saw that we were selling way more than his touring company was, so he was giving us a lot more opportunity to make it our own space. They still had a space to perform, but they didn't like that it was looked at as our home club."

Although he eventually agreed to drop the magician act, Riggs still insisted that the All-Stars conduct their residencies in the same way his other troupes did: by always creating new material. "Dudley added a caveat that we needed to create a show of all-new material," Madison says. "I think Louie suspected that early on, which was part of the reason why he wanted me and Jeff. He knew we were two guys

The Minneapolis Comedy All-Stars take a potshot at Minnesota Twins owner Calvin Griffith in an ad for their "championship-caliber" comedy revue.

who were hungry and wanted to eventually head somewhere beyond Minneapolis. So he knew we'd write and that we could show up with another twenty minutes of material every few weeks."

The group had two months off after its first run at the club before coming back for another eight to ten weeks. Cesario and Madison used that break to write and work on new material.

Not to be outdone, Cole was driven by the tenacity of the other All-Stars to up his game too. "Al saw that we were all writing a ton, so he got the hair up his ass to start coming up with new stuff too," Madison recalls. "We were all putting everything we had into it, and we made that All-Star name stick."

Cole remembers not only being motivated and inspired by his fellow All-Stars, but also the strong sense of camaraderie and partnership forged during their writing sessions. "The thing about working Dudley Riggs is that we weren't like LA or New York where comedians are trying to stick it to you—a real, 'I got mine, fuck you' type of attitude," Cole says. "The four of us got to work on each other's material. After every set Cesario would say, 'I got a tag for that bit,' and I'd say 'Great!' and then I'd work on it for the second show. I wrote material that I used for twenty-five years during those three years. It was an incredible way to learn. That's really how I learned my trade as a writer, working with those three guys."

Anderson echoes Cole's thoughts, and he credits the connection among the four original All-Stars for the show's success. "We just all got along," he says. "We kind of banded together like a band of brothers and created something new. Plus we were all different enough in our material where we weren't bleeding into each other."

Of course, the All-Stars weren't the only show in town when it came to stand-up. Mickey Finn's (now renamed Boomers) was still going strong, and the Comedy Cabaret was making a name for itself on the local scene, meaning there were plenty of opportunities for stage time for all comedians.

"The animosity that some of the comics had when we first started doing the All-Stars faded pretty fast," Madison says. "There was enough work for quality comics in town, so no one had trouble finding places to perform. The best comics made it regardless of where

The Minneapolis Comedy All-Stars: Jeff Cesario, Louie Anderson, Joel Madison, and Alex Cole (seated). (Courtesy of Joel Madison)

they performed. I even did a handful of open mics at Comedy Cabaret, so there really wasn't any bad blood between any of us in town."

"We were different from Hansen's room," Cole adds. "It gave audiences a really nice choice to see different kinds of comedy."

Everybody continued to adjust to the evolving landscape as well. After sixteen months and a nearly perfect record of sold-out shows with the Comedy All-Stars, Anderson decided to pack up and take his own show on the road. With the leader gone, the All-Stars carried on. "Louie left in the fall of '82, but we kept going with new shows, new titles, and new material," Cesario says.

Anderson's absence created an opening for a new fourth member, and another Mickey Finn's regular, John Heinz, was the first to fill that slot. "John was okay, but he just didn't really fit," Madison says. "Then Sid Youngers joined the group when he left, and Sid was great. He was really the only guy in town who was doing improv and stand-up and really great at both. He just got too busy, though."

Soon, the group added its first female member. Susan Vass, who had been mentored by Anderson, joined the group and helped take the All-Stars into 1983. That spring, they lost another core member when Cesario left town to pursue the next phase of his career out west.

The departures left a void not only from a performance standpoint but from a business perspective as well. "When Louie was around, he was in charge of speaking to Dudley," Madison recalls. "It was awesome. I knew Dudley a little bit because I'd been through his workshops, but he always scared the heck out of me. Just very intimidating. Once you got to know him, he was a pussycat, but to me he was this comedy legend. So when Louie left, Jeff agreed to take over being the one who talked to Dudley. Then when he left, I did it, and I basically decided that I'd rather quit comedy than keep doing that. I just didn't like the business end of it at all and didn't want that responsibility."

Madison lasted another two years with the All-Stars alongside Cole, Vass, and a handful of others who rotated in and out of the lineup. Eventually, he too felt the itch to take his show on the road and followed Cesario to California.

"They still had the name, but the gold had kind of tarnished a bit at that point from what I understand," says Madison of the remnants of the Minneapolis Comedy All-Stars.

Cole, who stayed with the group until the end, says that his bonds with the founding foursome benefited his career immensely. "The All-Stars were a unique situation. I'm the lamest one of the group," he says with a laugh. "I worked in Vegas, signed with ABC, and did really well for myself. But I wanted to stay in touch with those three [Anderson, Cesario, and Madison] because they were always doing something really great."

A few years later, Bill Bauer adopted the "Minneapolis Comedy All-Stars" name for a tour he did with another group of comedians.

Similarly, Anderson, Hansen, and Gerbino got back together in the early nineties for a reunion event and called themselves the Comedy All-Stars.

Still, the original All-Stars gang of Anderson, Cole, Cesario, and Madison is the one synonymous with bringing stand-up to Dudley Riggs and with bridging the divide between stand-up comedy and improv in Minneapolis.

"We put everything we had into those shows," Madison says. "We saw it as our opportunity to take the next step beyond just getting onstage for fun, and Louie is really the one who deserves the credit for making it possible."

Although he wasn't there for the entire run, Anderson says the All-Stars were a special group that not only helped him grow as a performer but helped raise all of their stock as comedians. "I felt like I was a part of something," he says. "I was part of a puzzle. I was very proud to be able to offer something unique to this picture of comedy at the time, and be a part of the puzzle we had put together. It was really historic for us, and it helped all of us get a little more credit."

••• 10 •••

The Birth of the Comedy Gallery

When Scott Hansen decided to make the move to J. R.'s Restaurant and open a new comedy club, he realized it was time to create a new comedy experience to go along with it.

"The Comedy Cabaret was still a cabaret," Hansen says. "There was juggling, sword swallowers, and musical acts. Then you had Mickey Finn's, where you could see a whole bunch of comics, but there wasn't really a structure. I decided to make my club the first real comedy club in Minneapolis."

Peter Staloch remembers the first time Hansen broached the idea of splitting off from the Cabaret and starting a new club: "In early 1982, Scott Hansen approached Lee [Schmidt] and me, feeling us out if we wanted to start a new comedy venue with him. He was in discussions with the owner of a restaurant downtown called J. R.'s. There was a space upstairs of the restaurant, where there was a bar, that would be a perfect venue for stand-up comedy."

The club had about a hundred seats in a room above J. R.'s on LaSalle Avenue North in Minneapolis. Hansen knew he had the right space, the right people, and the right audience. Now he just needed the right name for the outside of the building. "At our first meeting in the new downtown space, the task was to come up with a name for the club," recalls Staloch. "Something a bit more classy than Chuckles or HaHa's or Wacko's. We scoured our brains until Lee Schmidt finally came up with the perfect name: the Comedy Gallery. Descriptive and classy, it denoted a bit more sophistication and variety."

The stage at Scott Hansen's Comedy Gallery, located upstairs at J. R.'s Restaurant and Lounge. (Courtesy of Mike Gandolfi)

With the lease signed and the room ready, the Comedy Gallery opened in March 1982, and Hansen got to work creating buzz for the new club. He put up posters, contacted the local media, and placed full-page ads in the newspapers. "It was the first time I had been in touch with the media myself," Hansen says.

While he was new to being the face of a particular club, Hansen had a knack for promotion. The ads featured him pulled up at a dinner table, fork in hand, with the caption: "When Scott Hansen isn't eating at J. R.'s he's working there. Now that's funny."

"I knew I had to come up with ads that would get people's attention," he recalls. "Whether that meant using funny props or making fun of myself like that J. R.'s ad, I had to be different."

The Comedy Gallery had to be different, and it had to be good. Hansen brought with him a handful of the area's best performers to help get the club off the ground. Joel Hodgson, who had become the most talked about comic in town, became exclusive to the Gallery. Hansen also brought the comedy duo of Peter Staloch and Lee Schmidt, plus Jeff Schilling and Ron Douglas.

"Our club was the first to do the traditional lineup of an opener, a feature middle act, and a headliner," Hansen says. "The idea was to create structure for the audience, but also for the comics. Now if you were a comic, you knew that you could work as an opener and

Ad for Scott Hansen's Comedy Gallery at J. R.'s Restaurant

then work your way up to a middle and then a headliner and make more money."

The opening weekend was set for March 18–20. Hodgson and the tandem of Staloch and Schmidt were the first headliner and middle acts, respectively, in Comedy Gallery history. Hansen, who controlled the booking and arranging of talent, relegated himself to the role of emcee. "I didn't put myself up as a headliner for a very long time," he remembers. "I'd say the first two years I only emceed."

Billing itself as "The Premiere Comedy Nightclub," the Comedy Gallery was an instant success. Featuring talent that was seen as more polished than at Mickey Finn's and more focused than at the Cabaret, the shows routinely sold out.

"What followed was a parade of stand-ups, some already well honed in their chops, some still needing to work out their timing and their bits in clean, five-minute segments," says Staloch. "The Comedy Gallery became popular, because you could have dinner at J. R.'s and then come upstairs for drinks and a show."

Though Hansen moved the club away from the variety act stylings that had come through the Comedy Cabaret, he wasn't entirely opposed to mixing things up now and then. "We had this clown named T. C. Hatter," Hansen recalls. "Bauer refused to put him on at Mickey Finn's. He'd sit there and complain, 'I'm not putting some fucking clown onstage!' But he [the clown] was hilarious, and that was all I cared about. So I gave him the opportunity."

Hansen also began promoting group shows, similar to the model Louie Anderson and Dudley Riggs were using with the Minneapolis Comedy All-Stars. And Hansen didn't shy away from using creative and sometimes borderline offensive taglines to build buzz. "For me it was about finding a unique way to advertise the shows so people would notice," Hansen says. "For example, there was a comedy duo called Two Much and Company that was two black comedians. So we paired them up with T. C. Hatter and called the show 'Two Blacks and a Colored Guy.'"

Similarly, a group of comedians that included Steven Powell (an African American), Bruce Murray (a Native American), Joe Minjares

The opening weekend of the Comedy Gallery in March 1982 featured "comic magician" Joel Hodgson, the comedy duo of Staloch & Schmidt, and Scott Hansen.

Five of the six performers in the "Three Blacks, a Mexican, an Indian and a Jew Review": (clockwise from lower left) Steven Powell, Bruce Murray, Michael Jacobs, Joe Minjares, and Glenn Tanner

(a Latino), and others was packaged in a show entitled, "Three Blacks, a Mexican, an Indian and a Jew Review." "You certainly couldn't get away with naming shows like that these days," Hansen acknowledges.

Minjares, who owned the popular Pepito's Mexican restaurant in Minneapolis for many years, caught Hansen's eye around 1982 when he started performing at some of the open stages Hansen ran around town. Minjares was invited to be an emcee for some Comedy Gallery open mic nights, which brought him more attention and opportunities. "Scott called me one day and gave me the pitch [for 'Three Blacks, a Mexican, an Indian and a Jew Review']. He told me the title, and I thought it was great," Minjares recalls. "When you're doing a group show like that, it's really important to have a good title. Scott was great at coming up with those."

The show itself proved to be massively successful, selling out full weekend runs at the Comedy Gallery on a regular basis. While the title would certainly raise eyebrows today, Minjares says the controversial name actually diversified the club's audience. "It was a little bit of a dangerous name, right there on the edge," he says. "But it brought in a more diverse audience than we'd have on other nights at the club. It was a really smart idea."

Joe Minjares at Scott Hansen's Comedy Gallery. (Courtesy of Mike Gandolfi)

Another innovative move was that Hansen put the talent to work even when they weren't onstage. Everyone, including Hansen, was always working when they were in the club, whether it was taking tickets or ushering audience members to their seats. "We wanted people to enter laughing," Hansen says. "I wanted to set a tone right away that you were going to get a good show. Odds are if you came to one of our shows, for quite some time it was one of the comedians that night who would be seating you personally."

With shows Thursdays through Saturdays, Hansen was always hustling to put fresh talent onstage in order to keep customers coming back. Thursday nights were local talent showcases, branded "Catch a Rising Star" nights. Fridays and Saturdays were reserved for bigger, more well-established acts, both local and national.

While the open mic night was a proving ground for many locals who would go on to become marquee names at the Comedy Gallery as well as at other clubs around town, plenty of less impressive performers came and went without their star rising. Ken Bradley, who worked for Hansen and became a regular emcee of the open mic night, recalls more than one would-be comic who was memorable for all the wrong reasons. "There was one guy that we used to call the Snatch Comic," Bradley recalls. "He was a scary dude who would show up to the open stage, and every one of his jokes would end with, 'And then I grabbed her in the snatch!' And it was not funny, and it made everyone uncomfortable. To his credit, Scott would still let him up, but he'd tell me to give him the light [comic-speak for telling someone that their time is up]. I'd give him the light, and he wouldn't get off. So I'd be sneaking up onstage to the point I'd be standing next to him trying to take the mic out of his hand. It was so offensive."

Rick Carney, another regular in Hansen's lineup as an emcee, also frequently had a front-row seat for the cringeworthy newbies. People were usually fairly polite in the face of these less polished performers, but Carney remembers one night when Alex Cole lost his cool over an open mic-er. "I remember this guy, David Foss, and he would get onstage with a banjo, and all his jokes were written on note cards," Carney recalls with a laugh. "I never saw him play the banjo, and he'd read his jokes right off the cards. So you would be trying to give him the light to get him off the stage, and he wouldn't even look up."

Carney explains that it was kind of an unspoken rule at the time that if a comic like Alex Cole or Tom Arnold or someone at that level came in and wanted to go onstage to work on jokes during an open mic night, they could go right up and stay on for as long as they wanted. "One night Alex came in while David Foss was onstage," Carney continues, "and he's waiting and he's waiting, and finally David gets off and Alex goes on. After about nine minutes, the guy who was working the light for us that night flashed it, telling Alex he only had a minute left. Alex went ballistic. He's screaming, 'Fuck you with that light! I had to watch that fucking note card guy! I'll go as long as I fucking want to!' It wasn't David Foss's fault, but it was just funny to hear him get called out like that. I don't think he showed up at another open stage after that night."

Another performer who never quite made it out of the first gear of his comedy career was a guy named Gomez O'Prey. "Gomez was another interesting character," Bradley remembers. "He worked for Scott tearing tickets and doing some other things. Gomez was in charge of driving around the headliners who would come into town, and he would try to pattern himself after them. Whoever was the headliner the week prior is what Gomez's act would be the next. So if Will Durst, who did political stuff, performed one week, the next week Gomez would do political stuff."

Carney says he didn't even know O'Prey was a comic—despite the fact he saw him onstage more than once before performing himself. "The first time I ever went to the Comedy Gallery, me and my girlfriend went to see Bill Bauer," Carney recalls. "Gomez was the emcee, and he'd come out and talk and bring people up. The next time I was there was actually to perform for the open stage, and I followed Gomez. He came offstage and I said, 'You're a comic too?' I thought he was just sort of the house announcer who told you where to get drinks and how things worked."

Ron Douglas, who had been one of Hansen's most reliable comics, was the first black performer to headline the Comedy Gallery.

Lizz Winstead, who went on to have a tremendous impact both as a performer and as a mentor to other women in town, was the first female comedian to headline. Gerry Bednob, the only comedian from Bangladesh touring in the United States, performed there and presented a picture of life that had never been seen or heard on most American stages, let alone in Minnesota. Hansen brought him to the club within the first few months as a headliner. And, naturally, one of the most popular headliners who performed at the club was Louie Anderson.

Anderson had begun to make a name for himself out west, with appearances on *The Tonight Show* and regular slots at the Improv. Still, when Anderson came to the Comedy Gallery, he considered it a homecoming. "I was very proud of my success," he says. "And I was still very much a hometown guy. I really loved Minnesota, and I considered the success I had all of our [the original five's] success in a way. The public picks who is going to be the most popular and most successful, unfortunately. It's just how life works. But I got to where I was because of their help, and when I would come back I wanted the same for them."

Audiences also considered Anderson a homegrown star whenever he returned to perform at Hansen's room. He admits his level of fame was noticeable among his peers, which might have created tension. "I probably thought I was a big shot in some ways," he says. "I hope I wasn't an asshole to anyone. When you become successful, it automatically takes you into another space. It just happens. But I never forgot the guys I started with, and I wanted to send some light their way. I don't think anyone came back to perform as much as I did."

While the Comedy Gallery stage presented plenty of familiar faces to audiences, the club was progressive in embracing new talents and concepts. Hansen produced female-led shows, like when comedian (and later daytime talk show host) Jenny Jones came to perform at the club. She made her event an all-women show, and men were not allowed to attend. Even all the servers and bartenders for the evening were women.

Hansen was also one of the first promoters to bring in openly gay performers, though one night he didn't know that's what he was

*Bill Bauer, Louie Ander-
son, and Alex Cole at Scott
Hansen's Comedy Gallery.
(Courtesy of Mike Gandolfi)*

*Scott Hansen, Bill Bauer, Alex
Cole, and Louie Anderson at
the Comedy Gallery. (Courtesy of Mike Gandolfi)*

doing ahead of time. "Sometimes we'd only get maybe ten or fifteen people at our open mic nights," Hansen remembers. "One night we had like a hundred people in the audience, which was pretty unusual. Sometimes we'd have a new guy who would come in and bring a bunch of friends, and that's what this particular night was. So this guy gets up onstage and says, 'I've got a nephew named Billy, and Billy asked me the other day, Uncle Jack, you have an earring in your ear. Does that make you gay? And I told him, no Billy, the fact that I like to suck cocks makes me gay.' Then he looks at the front row and says, 'Mom, Dad, Grandma, Grandpa—I'm a homosexual.' People literally ran out of the room crying. He had his entire family there, and he decided this was how he was going to come out. By the time he got offstage, there were thirteen people left in the audience."

By September of 1982, Hansen had another idea that would not only secure the Comedy Gallery's place as the number one comedy club in Minneapolis but put it on the map as one of the most talent-heavy clubs in the entire country. In a circle-of-life moment that brought Hansen back to his roots, he decided to host a comedy contest. But unlike the Mickey Finn's competition five years earlier, this competition would have much higher stakes.

The first-annual Twin Cities Comedy Invitational brought together comedians from all over the country for a two-week competition featuring a $500 grand prize. "I was the only comic with a good enough credit rating to get some money to put on this thing," Hansen said in an interview with the *Twin Cities Reader* leading up to the big throw down.

Another aspect of this contest that was very different from the one at Finn's was that the talent was screened and narrowed down ahead of time, and contestants were placed into different divisions based on

Two of the Class A competitors in the first annual Twin Cities Comedy Invitational will be Houstonian Jeff Schilling, left, who is called the "one-man crowd" because of his multiple characterizations, and mimeclown T.C. Hatter, known for involving his audience in the fun.

Comedians: Thrive on competition

Jeff Schilling (left) and T. C. Hatter (right) were two of the participants in the inaugural Twin Cities Comedy Invitational in September 1982. (From the St. Paul Dispatch*)*

experience. This was similar to how bigger contests were structured in Los Angeles, St. Louis, or Chicago, where some of the original five were beginning to build reputations. Louie Anderson, for example, had taken third place in a contest in St. Louis the year prior, finishing behind a singer and a clown. Jeff Gerbino had recently made it to the finals of the Los Angeles Comedy Contest.

For the Comedy Gallery competition, comedians were put into Class AA, the more polished and professional group, if they had won or been a finalist in a competition before. This group included Gerbino, along with fellow original Alex Cole, local breakout Joel Hodgson, Chicago comics Frank Hooper and Ed Fiala, and Jeff Wayne, who came in from Los Angeles.

The Class A group was for comics who had performed in a previous competition, been recommended by a trusted performer, or been seen often enough and considered talented enough by Hansen himself. Among the comics in this group were Frank Poynton from Chicago and Jeff Schilling from Houston, who submitted videotapes to Hansen in order to get into the competition. They were joined by some familiar faces from around town, including Jeff Cesario, Bruce Murray, Staloch & Schmidt, Two Much and Company, and T. C. Hatter, to name a few. Right away, Hansen was proud to see how seriously the acts were taking his contest.

"Being in a comedy contest looked good on a résumé," he said in an interview about the competition. "It helped Louie, and I already booked the guy who had finished ahead of him to perform at the Comedy Gallery. Plus, it was a chance for the crowds to see the acts at their best. It was the very best fifteen minutes they had to offer, because they had something to shoot for."

The competition kicked off with preliminary rounds at the Comedy Gallery and at a bar called Crocus Cabana, located on Grand Avenue in St. Paul. Over the course of the next several days, the contestants would perform six times for hand-selected judges encompassing members of the media, talent agency representatives, and comedy patrons who graded competitors on the quality of the material, stage presence, and audience response. When the dust settled,

Hodgson had won the title and the prize money at the inaugural Comedy Gallery competition, securing his place as a bona fide home-grown comedy star.

Hansen continued the competition for several more years, and it got more and more hotly contested. "I actually won the contest one year," Minjares says. "But once I had won, especially as a newer comedian in a group with a lot of more experienced guys, it definitely started to become more competitive. It also opened a lot of doors for me, because it allowed me to start opening for some of the national acts that Scott was bringing in."

The national acts Minjares mentions were coming through the Comedy Gallery thanks to the club's growing reputation with comedy bookers, talent agents, and comedians. But Hansen wasn't content to simply sit back and let the talent come to him. Instead, he hit the road and found talent in other cities that he thought would be a good fit for audiences back in Minnesota.

"I liked to get out of town and perform in Chicago sometimes," Hansen recalls. "And I found so many acts there that I knew the Minneapolis crowds would go crazy for." One of the first was a woman named Judy Tenuta.

Armed with an accordion, a tiara, and a sharp enough tongue to hang with any crowd, Tenuta billed herself as "unofficially one of the top accordionists in the country." Her tongue-in-cheek megalomania and twisted take on traditionally tame topics made her a regular fixture of the Chicago club scene before Hansen saw her perform at the same club where he was performing on a rare travel weekend. "She was incredible," says Hansen. "I had never seen anyone like her. I knew if I wanted to make the Comedy Gallery different, I needed to find acts no one had seen before, and Judy was a hit the first time she performed at the club."

Another comic Hansen discovered during a trip to Chicago was Emo Philips. Today regarded as a pioneer of alt-comedy, with his unconventional presentation and personality, Philips was onstage one night in Chicago, performing for a crowd of about twenty people, when Hansen first laid eyes on him. And it almost didn't happen.

As Tom Hansen recalls: "I got a call from Scott that his car broke

Judy Tenuta at Scott Hansen's Comedy Gallery. (Courtesy of Mike Gandolfi)

down in Eau Claire, Wisconsin, so I had to go pick him up, along with a comedian named Bruce Murray, and drive them to Chicago to a club called Who's On First? ... We get to the club in Chicago, and it's completely flooded. It's underwater. So another comic suggested we go to a one-nighter they had in a Catholic church down the road. I watched Emo onstage for over an hour, playing around with a trombone. The entire time he was onstage, he kept taking this trombone apart and putting it back together, and he never played a note."

Like much of the crowd that night, Tom was blown away by Philips's performance. Scott saw the potential to bring Emo to a brand-new audience. "I thought to myself, Minnesota is going to love this guy," Hansen recalls. "I talked to him after the show, and he stayed in character one hundred percent. So I got him to Minneapolis, and the town loved him. Only problem is that I'm paying him $350 for the week, and he can't afford a hotel. So I let him stay with me and my family in our little house in Minneapolis."

Emo Philips onstage at Scott Hansen's Comedy Gallery. (Photo by Donald Black, Minneapolis Tribune, from the Minnesota Historical Society Collections)

With one child at home and another on the way, Hansen and his wife, Michelle, were hesitant about allowing a performer into their home. But with few other options, they reluctantly welcomed in Philips. It would be the last time Hansen let a comic stay with him.

"Emo has this thing where he likes to test his character on people and see how far he can push it," Hansen says. "I didn't know that until I talked to Judy Tenuta a few weeks later. I was just like, 'That would have been something you could have mentioned.'"

One day, Hansen came home to find Philips standing in his front yard playing the trombone on the lawn while neighbors and passersby looked on in confusion. Another time, Philips and Hansen were in the kitchen when Philips asked if he could make an egg. "I didn't think anything of it at first, which was my mistake," Hansen says with a sigh. "He takes out a skillet and throws an entire raw egg into the pan, smashing it. Then he's sitting there flicking the shells out onto the floor. I let him go for a minute before I said, 'Emo, do you know how to make an egg?' And in that real high-pitched voice he goes, 'I guess not, Scott.' Eventually, I found out that you had to say, 'Hey, Phil'—which is his real name—'stop being Emo,' and then he would drop the character. Otherwise, he was always in character. He did that because he was always writing. It was brilliant, but it made me want to kill him at first."

Although he may not have been welcome as a houseguest, Philips became a regular at the Comedy Gallery before and during his rise to fame. He was also responsible for one unique differentiator of the club. "We were the first club in town, and maybe the country, that was completely smoke free," Hansen says. "It started with Emo. He was so allergic to the smoke that we did away with it when he came to town, and people really enjoyed it, so we kept it that way."

Hansen's eye for talent was incredible, but that isn't to say that every act connected with audiences. "I brought in this comedy duo, Leo Benvenuti and Steve Rudnick, who had been part of Second City [in Chicago]. They got the worst review in the history of the club," he says with a laugh. "Not a single person laughed. Finally, someone stood up and said, 'You're too smart!' You probably wouldn't know those names until I tell you about what they went on to do. They wrote a lot of films like *The Santa Clause, Space Jam,* and *Kicking & Screaming.*"

One name from Hansen's Comedy Cabaret past also became a regular at his new club. Tom Arnold was a frequent part of the evening lineup at the Comedy Gallery. In fact, that's where he met Roseanne Barr. "We managed to book Roseanne for $350 for the week," Hansen remembers. "She had opened for me at Comedy Works in Denver. The minute she walked off the stage, I hired her for the Comedy Gallery."

After booking Barr, he called Arnold. He told him he had a "woman headliner, Jewish comic from Denver," and he thought Arnold would be perfect for the middle spot. The following week, the couple met at the Comedy Gallery, and they got together soon after. Both Hansen and the club would be depicted in the 1994 made-for-TV movie produced at the peak of Barr and Arnold's fame, *Roseanne and Tom: Behind the Scenes.*

Roseanne Barr and Tom Arnold at Scott Hansen's Comedy Gallery at Galtier Plaza in St. Paul. (Courtesy of Scott Hansen)

Not only would the Comedy Gallery bring the comedy power couple together; it also opened the door for other comedians whom Arnold and Barr invited out to work with them later in California.

After featuring a handful of up-and-comers and comics on the cusp of stardom, Hansen finally booked his first major act—at the suggestion of his mother. "My mom calls me one day and says, 'You know who you should use at your club?' and I'm rolling my eyes, like I'm going to take comedy tips from my mother. She says, 'Jay Leno.' At that point, he hadn't even done Carson yet. He was just hitting his stride on David Letterman's daytime talk show, which my mother watched all the time."

Despite his initial skepticism, Hansen looked into Leno and decided to bring him in for a two-night engagement. "It was $7,500 to get him for two nights, which at that point was more money than I had ever spent in my entire life," Hansen remembers. "It was like one-fourth of the cost of my first house."

COMING!COMING!

FEB. 8-12

Tickets at Dayton's
or Comedy Gallery

JAY LENO

THE COMEDY GALLERY
UPSTAIRS AT JR'S RESTAURANT
11th & LaSalle, Mpls.
Dining, Cocktails, Comedy
338-2424

THE COMEDY GALLERY

NO RESERVATIONS — NO COUPONS

A flyer for Jay Leno's first visit to Scott Hansen's Comedy Gallery in Minneapolis

Much to Hansen's delight, his mother's intuition was correct. "We were supposed to have him for Wednesday and Thursday, and we sold out both shows. So then we added a Friday show and sold that out. Then we added a Saturday show and sold that out too. We decided to add a Sunday show."

Hansen's big gamble was paying off, but he narrowly avoided a potential disaster involving Dayton's department store, which was selling tickets for the shows. "They accidentally sold double the tickets they were supposed to for the Sunday show," Hansen recalls. "We called Leno's agent, expecting to either have to refund a bunch of people or pay him a ton of money. Leno said, 'Let's just add a second show for Sunday.' And he agreed to work for the same amount of money. He could have easily said, 'You fucked up, so you're going to give me a hundred percent of the door.' But he didn't. He knew I supported him and found incentives to help him make money, so he supported me right back."

Leno's flexibility was a welcome relief for Hansen, who says the future talk show host's amicable personality was on display all week. "One night I'm coming downstairs to the restaurant, and I see Jay carrying a woman up the stairs," Hansen recalls. "She had crutches and he insisted on helping her up. That's just the kind of guy he was."

The Leno gig also helped Hansen to showcase his own comedian-friendly outlook and business acumen, which made him a hit with bookers and helped give the Comedy Gallery a strong national reputation. "Once Leno played at our club, a couple of weeks later we got a call from Jerry Seinfeld's manager. He had heard good things and wanted to come in. We had people calling us because they knew we paid well and we were going to treat them well."

Seinfeld made his Comedy Gallery debut in the fall of 1985. At the time, he was a regular guest of Carson and Letterman but was still several years away from sitcom superstardom. Crowds packed the Gallery for six shows across three nights, shelling out eight dollars a ticket along with a mandatory two-beverage minimum for the opportunity to see the comic dig beneath the surface of everyday observational comedy. A review in the *Minneapolis Star and Tribune* called Seinfeld, "pulverizingly funny, without stooping to the slurs,

Scott Hansen and Jerry Seinfeld at Scott Hansen's Comedy Gallery. (Courtesy of Mike Gandolfi)

put-downs and profanity to which less talented performers resort." It would be his first of many visits to the Twin Cities and the beginning of a long relationship between himself and Hansen.

Seinfeld's connection to the club also helped to steer the careers of many Comedy Gallery regulars, including Joel Hodgson. As Seinfeld's opener, Hodgson was able to showcase his deadpan style and unconventional approach, and the two became fast friends. They have frequently performed together, and Hodgson appeared on the first season of Seinfeld's web series, *Comedians in Cars Getting Coffee.*

Joe Minjares was another comedian whose life was changed by Seinfeld's affinity for the Comedy Gallery. "When I opened for Seinfeld, it was my wedding anniversary that same night," Minjares recalls. "I opened for Jerry and did very well, and then my wife and I went downstairs to J. R.'s for dinner. A few minutes later, the waiter brings by a bottle of wine signed by Seinfeld saying 'happy anniversary.'"

A nice bottle of wine was just one way Minjares benefited from the connection. "A year later, I was walking down Melrose in Hollywood, and I see Seinfeld walking toward me with Larry David. I kind of figured he wouldn't remember me, but as we got closer he smiled, and I waved to him. He stops and says, 'Joe Minjares. Larry, this is Joe Minjares from Minneapolis.' He asked me what I was doing out there, and I told him I was looking to get into more television and film roles. He got me an audition for his show, and when I got there, he said, 'You're not reading. You've got the part.' He just gave me the role right there on the spot."

Meanwhile, back in the Twin Cities, the Comedy Gallery was lapping its competition. "Mickey Finn's didn't bring in anybody," Hansen says. "And the Cabaret was bringing in out-of-town acts, but they were still more of a variety show. I was really the only one bringing in big names from all over the country on a regular basis."

Rob Schneider, Larry Miller, and Bill Hicks would all grace the Comedy Gallery stage in the years following. All the while, Hansen continued to grow as a comic. "I would book whoever I thought was the best comic to open for certain acts," he says. "If I thought I was the best fit, I would book myself. I put myself with Leno and a few others, but in general I was trying to get in one show a week."

The Comedy Gallery at J. R.'s was the hottest ticket in town. In fact, it had become too big for its current home. Hansen needed to think bigger once again. It was time for the Comedy Gallery to grow.

··· 11 ···

The Arrival of Louis Lee

One night in 1981, as the Minneapolis Comedy All-Stars were hitting their stride at Dudley Riggs's ETC, there was a young man in the audience named Louis Lee. Then aged twenty-three, Lee had moved to the United States from Hong Kong four years earlier to attend college at the University of Minnesota.

Although Lee had been in the country for a few years already, he was still working on learning to speak English and how to fit in as an American. "I used to go to the theater and watch one movie every week to learn a little bit more English," he recalls. "I could read and write in English, but day-to-day conversation was a lot different. Plus, everyone I worked with was American, and sometimes it was hard for me to follow what they were saying."

However, the language barrier didn't stop him from heading to the comedy club and having an experience that would change his life forever. "I had my first American girlfriend that year," Lee says. "One night she told me, 'You're working really hard to fit in, and I think there's something you should see.' She took me to the show where it was Alex Cole, Louie Anderson, Jeff Cesario, and Joel Madison. I only understood about half of the show, but the crowd was just so good. I was looking around and thinking, 'This is how people communicate with each other.' It was different than reading or writing English. It was different from movies too. Those were very scripted, and this just felt like people talking naturally."

Aside from the manner of the dialogue, Lee was also taken aback by the energy in the room. "It was like five or six bucks to get in, and there were a ton of people my age," he says. "Everyone just wanted to relax and drink a beer and watch the show. I was thinking, 'This is how I can learn more English, and I can be funny when I talk to other people, by stealing the jokes from the comics.'"

Beginning with that night, Lee fell in love with comedy. He soaked up as much stand-up as he could, whenever and wherever he could. "I'd go to a lot of comedy shows," he says. "I'd go to Dudley Riggs, but I also went down to Mickey Finn's and Williams—anywhere I could."

For his day job, Lee was working at a Chinese restaurant off of Interstate 494 in Minneapolis called Mandarin Yen. An enormous space, the restaurant and bar sat hundreds, and an adjoining banquet room could fit upward of three hundred people. The restaurant was in a high-traffic area, and competition among the bars and restaurants was pretty intense.

"I started as a host, and very quickly they moved me up to assistant manager," Lee says. "At the time, the owner, a guy named Frank Lee [no relation] just followed whatever was working. He had a band that would play Top 40 songs in the bar. So I told him, 'You're spending too much money on entertainment. Every bar on 494 has a Top 40 band, so you can't charge a cover because nobody else is.' I told him we needed to find another type of entertainment to be unique and stand out, and I suggested we try stand-up comedy."

The finances made sense. Lee, who had been to at least ten or fifteen comedy shows by then, recognized that stand-up was booming and that the bar could easily get as many patrons to come in for comedy as for music, but without the expense of having to pay a band. Frank Lee was skeptical, but he was open to any idea that resulted in him making fast cash. So he let Louis explore the option.

"I told some of my buddies that I had talked my boss into giving comedy a try, and they told me I should call Scott Hansen," Lee remembers. "They said he would probably be interested in listening to the idea and might be willing to help. I looked up the number for the Comedy Gallery and gave him a call, and he came out to take a look."

Hansen was intrigued by the space but was concerned about the restaurant's proximity to another popular comedy venue, the Carlton Celebrity Room. "Scott didn't want to make enemies with the Carlton, so he said why don't we try improv first?" Lee says. "So I let Scott book the talent, and he took the door. Right away, it was working. It wasn't huge, but we were still pulling in the same amount of people and saving a lot of money."

The room eventually grew to include stand-up, and much like Lee had anticipated, it started to build a following. Unfortunately, it wasn't enough for his boss. "Frank was mad because the money wasn't coming in fast enough," he says. "I remember one day he came in and he was just in a foul mood, and he snapped at me for having three busboys working instead of cutting someone. I heard that and thought, 'Seriously? He's yelling at me, and I'm saving him a huge amount of money.' And he's still paying me $14,000 a year, working seven days a week. So I decided that I didn't need this anymore, and I walked out on Frank."

While Louis knew it was time to leave Mandarin Yen, he didn't have a backup plan. Fortunately, Lee soon found himself working at a restaurant on St. Anthony Main in Minneapolis, near Riverplace Plaza. The restaurant was owned by Rick Janucz, whom Lee had connected with through his many years in the industry. Lee recognized Janucz's knack for running successful businesses and looked to him as a potential investor. Soon, Lee had developed a new idea for a comedy club.

"The second floor of Riverplace Plaza had been empty for years," Lee recalls. "The owners of the building had this great idea one summer. They said, 'Let's do summer theater.' They built a big stage and a really nice space, but the whole thing fell apart and just sat there. So I had the idea to go in and do stand-up comedy there. And I knew just who to turn to."

By that time, the Comedy Gallery had outgrown its space above J. R.'s Restaurant. Not that it wasn't still a fantastic venue for comedy—even after Hansen left, the room was rebranded and served as more of an open stage showcase for local comics to work on their sets, while crowds could still enjoy a night of comedy with their dinners—but for the caliber of acts Hansen was promoting at the time, and the growing demand of crowds for live comedy, the need for a larger space was apparent.

So when Lee called Hansen and invited him to take a look at this new room at Riverplace, the timing couldn't have been better. Hansen saw the size of the space, the custom-built stage, and the prime location. The decision was clear. Hansen ended his longtime partnership with J. R.'s, and in the fall of 1987, Comedy Gallery Riverplace was open for business. The deal among Lee, Janucz, and Hansen was clear-cut: Lee and Janucz would run the bar, and Hansen would manage the comedy and take the money from the door. Almost overnight, the new space was a tremendous success.

"We opened the week of the World Series, and the place was booming," Lee remembers. "That space hadn't been touched in four and a half years, and all of a sudden it's packed. I remember Scott brought in Roseanne Barr and Tom Arnold that year to perform on New Year's Day and the day after, and sold it out. To sell out on New Year's Day is incredible."

Given that the space had been somewhat cursed prior to the Comedy Gallery moving in, Lee and Hansen struck a deal with the landlord to pay what's known as a percentage rent. That meant they would be on a month-to-month deal, and they would pay a total of six percent of all ticket and alcohol sales to the landlord—the idea being that if they were successful, everyone was successful. But when you have the kind of success the Comedy Gallery was enjoying, big businesses with deeper pockets tend to start sniffing around.

"A company approached the landlord about turning that space into a nightclub," Lee says. "So the building's owner offered us a deal. He told us he'd sell us the historic building that was in front of our space. It was a three-story building and had a different layout than our old Riverplace building. He told us he thought the future was brewpubs, and we could build a brewery in the basement, have a restaurant on the main floor, and then turn the top floor into a comedy club. For Scott, he knew it was either do this or lose his club six months in and go crawling back to J. R.'s. So we became partners in a brewpub."

The new space was an ideal location for the entrepreneurs, but it came with a hefty price tag. The building price was about $1.3 million, though Riverplace gave them $400,000 for improvements. Hansen and Lee would have to come up with roughly $800,000. Lee, who had built a solid reputation on the success of his restaurant projects, went in search of investors. In the end, they borrowed a ton of money, at a steep eighteen percent interest rate. Nevertheless, things moved forward, and in 1989, the new Comedy Gallery Riverplace was open for business.

Much like the previous location, the entire operation was successful right out of the gate. Hansen had booking and managing comedy down to a science, and Lee's skills managing the bar and restaurant made the club an immediate success. "Business was booming," Lee recalls. "The money was coming in fast, but we still had huge debt."

Not long after the new Comedy Gallery Riverplace opened, Hansen was approached by another comedian who had a tip on how to replicate the success of his club across the river in St. Paul. "There was a place in Galtier Plaza [in downtown St. Paul], and they wanted to do the same thing we had done with Riverplace," Lee recalls. "Brewery in the basement, restaurant, and then a comedy club upstairs."

Although they had proven the concept could succeed, Hansen was skeptical, due to the debt they had racked up opening their first location. "Scott said no way," Lee says. "He said he thought we owed way too much money already. I said, 'Look, let's just go check it out and see what they have to say.'"

The space was exactly what they would need for a new location. But what really interested Lee were the financial terms Galtier Plaza was offering. "Galtier was willing to give us $800,000 for improvements, and another $800,000 at an interest rate of four percent," Lee recalls. "We were paying eighteen percent at Riverplace, so my thought was we use the money to pay off Riverplace, and take the lower interest rate to pay down our total debt. The money worked."

Lee went to Hansen and explained that the math made sense, and that he believed they would be profitable very quickly. Hansen still wasn't convinced. "I told him he didn't have a choice," Lee adds with a laugh. "We had to do it. Eventually Scott agreed."

Lee soon began negotiating the lease on the Galtier Plaza space. At the same time, money had become so tight due to the Riverplace debt that Lee wasn't cashing his paychecks, and he had accumulated upward of $15,000 in unclaimed salary. "We needed money to cover payroll," he says plainly. "So I called my personal banker and said I needed him to float me the money to cover payroll, and I'd give him my paychecks to borrow against. He agreed, and told me to drive up and see him in North Branch and he'd take care of it."

Unfortunately for Lee, tragedy struck on the drive. A truck pushed his car off the road, causing a major accident. Lee was rushed to the hospital, and doctors contacted his business partners. "They said I had a serious head injury, and that they should call my family because I probably wasn't going to make it," he says.

Miraculously, twenty-four hours after that call, Lee regained consciousness. His head had been smashed in the accident, yet doctors were able to put his skull back together. Even more miraculous, there was no internal bleeding. Lee's face was temporarily paralyzed on one side, but otherwise he was fine. He was discharged from the hospital four days later.

Although he had managed to dodge death, Lee would soon find that his world had been changed forever. "When I was in the hospital for those four or five days, a major panic button was pushed," says Lee. "Scott was worried. He was thinking that he already owes $800,000, and now Louis got me in for another $800,000. And now Louis might be a vegetable. So if he dies, what the hell do I do?"

According to Lee, Hansen acted fast. His solution was to diminish Lee's role in the company while secretly having a discussion with Galtier Plaza to significantly dial back the expansion plans. All of this was unknown to Lee, who was kept in the dark during his recovery. In his mind, the plan that he had put in motion prior to his accident was still unfolding.

Right after New Year's, Hansen went to Lee and informed him that they needed $150,000 to show the St. Paul Port Authority, in order to move forward with their project. Not wanting to see everything he had worked for go by the wayside, Lee reluctantly reached out to his family in Hong Kong to borrow the money. "My family believed in me," Lee says. "They had seen the success I'd had up until that point in other restaurants, so they agreed to let me borrow the money in order to move ahead on the project."

Lee informed Hansen that he had secured the money and that all systems were go to proceed. Then, a month later, it all came crashing down. "Scott calls a meeting and says we need to pull back," Lee recalls. "He said we needed to scrap the restaurant and the brewpub, because we were already in too much debt. He also told me he was going to keep the comedy club piece but was going to do that part on his own."

Lee was upset by this development, but that was nothing compared to the next bomb Hansen dropped. "He also told me that I should work without pay at the restaurant in Minneapolis to help pay down our debt, since it had been my idea to put this whole thing together," Lee says. "Now I'm sitting here thinking, 'Wait, you just asked me to borrow money from my family, then you scrap the idea to make your side more profitable. That doesn't work.'"

Hansen was undeterred and called for a vote among the three partners, including Janucz. By a vote of two to one, Lee was removed from the business entirely. Lee was angry, shocked, and scared. "I told Scott I'd walk away, but he had better not mess with my family's money," Lee says. In order to keep the money Lee's family had lent intact, it would be up to Hansen and Janucz to make payments on their guaranteed loan to the bank. However, thirty days after removing Lee from the group, the remaining partners quit paying the loan, and the bank took the money from Lee's family.

"Now I've lost the money, and Scott has the business. He told me if I tried to mess with them, they would put the company into Chapter 11 and I'd be forced to lose even more. So that's how I managed to lose hundreds of thousands of dollars."

While Lee's version of the story paints Hansen in a less-than-desirable light, Hansen remembers things very differently. "Louis had money financed differently than he told us," Hansen says. "He had partners in the business whom he told would be paid back large sums of money. Meanwhile, he hasn't paid rent or sales tax. Then he got in the accident."

According to Hansen, neither he nor Janucz had any knowledge of Lee's alleged plan to get cash to cover payroll. "He had $15,000 in cash in the car with him at the time of the accident, in one of our bank bags, and he's coming from a bank where we don't have any accounts," Hansen recalls.

After the accident, Hansen says several new revelations came to light. "Louis's parents were involved with the tong in China, and they had guaranteed $250,000 in loans to him," he says. The tong were secret societies among Chinese immigrants living in the United States, usually with ties to criminal activity. In the late eighties and early nineties, most American Chinatowns were marked as tong halls, and many were known to have affiliations with Chinese crime gangs. This was a pretty serious allegation by Hansen, and one that Lee says was completely untrue.

"In order to have a license to open a brewpub in the eighties, all license holders—including myself—had to go through a BATF [Bureau of Alcohol, Tobacco, and Firearms] background check," Lee explains. "It was a long process because I am from Hong Kong. They also had all my family background as well. And after all that, I was granted the brewery license. I think Hansen's statement regarding Chinese immigrants in the US pretty much sums up his character and worldview."

Questions about Lee's family history aside, Hansen believes Lee wasn't truthful when it came to the club's finances. "When we got into business, I used my club as equity, and the other guy [Janucz] had a business he could use as equity," says Hansen. "Louis had a bank note. Then we found out he was taking a salary out of that bank note, and the company was paying interest on it. So he's living off of that money, and we're paying the interest. It was very convoluted."

With his name literally on the building proclaiming "Scott Hansen's Comedy Gallery," Hansen says he had no choice but to fire Lee in order to avoid filing for bankruptcy and ruining his own reputation. "I paid off $750,000 in creditors on my own," Hansen says.

Scott's brother Tom, who had taken over management duties for the comedy room at Mandarin Yen after Lee left, was also closely involved in the Comedy Gallery Riverplace business. He says he believes not only that Lee wronged his brother but that Lee was looking for a much more extreme way out. "Louis says it was a car accident, but I believe it was more of a suicide attempt," Hansen says. "He had gotten himself into too much trouble working underhandedly behind our backs, and he left Scott hanging with this bill from Riverplace. That's what happened there, and that's what caused our issue with Louis."

The true story of who screwed whom is still hotly contested, and Hansen and Lee have not spoken to each other since the dispute all those years ago. While Hansen's businesses continued to grow, Lee decided to leave comedy forever—at least, he thought it would be forever.

"I owed my family so much money," Lee recalls. "I got a job in a restaurant and didn't want to touch comedy. I remember thinking I could either try to find a way to pay back the money, or I could kill myself. I decided I wasn't going to do that, so what else could I do to repay the debt?"

In an ironic callback of sorts, Lee eventually found his way back into comedy, much like Hansen had years before.

... **12** ...

The Hansen Comedy Empire

Despite the controversy and conflicts surrounding the arrangement between Scott Hansen and Louis Lee, the Comedy Gallery locations in Minneapolis and St. Paul could not have been hotter in the early 1990s. Hansen had managed to take the next step as a businessman by establishing not just one, but two comedy venues that had the best possible stages, seating, lighting, and sound. Much in the way that venues like First Avenue are tailored for live music and the Guthrie for theater, Hansen created the equivalent for stand-up comedy.

The club at Riverplace in Minneapolis was unlike anything the local comedy world had seen to that point, and it was able to attract a regular flow of talent to keep it filled nearly every night of the week.

John Bush, a comedian who got his start around 1989, became a regular emcee and feature act at the new club, and he was blown away by the amenities. "Here's the thing about Scott Hansen," he says. "Nobody made better comedy clubs than he did. That Riverplace was the greatest comedy room I've ever been in. It had this amphitheater setup and was just built for comedy. It was the greatest room you could ever play."

Much like he had at his original Comedy Gallery location above J. R.'s steakhouse, Hansen brought in major names that could fill the massive space. True to form, however, the Riverplace club wasn't just about bringing in big names. It was a place where local talent could cut their teeth and gain valuable exposure as Hansen worked on cultivating the next generation of comics.

Alex Jackson was a firefighter by day and a regular part of the next group of up-and-coming comics who were hitting the stages popping up around town for open mic nights. The most notable of these stages was at Pepitos in south Minneapolis, owned by longtime Hansen associate Joe Minjares.

"There was a core group of us," Jackson remembers. "Myself, Ken Bradley, Eugene Meaux, Fancy Ray McCloney, and a few others. We'd route it so we could hit as many open stages as we could, and then always end up at Pepitos. Back then the name of the game was to work on your act in the smaller rooms and then try to get into the Comedy Gallery. That was the goal."

Unlike many others, Jackson didn't find his way into Hansen's clubs through the standard system of setting up chairs, taking tickets, and kissing the ring. Instead, he got in front of Hansen thanks to his relationship with Minjares. "One night I was performing at Pepitos, and Joe saw me," Jackson recalls. "He came up and told me, 'Do you know how funny you are? You are scary funny. Can I teach you to do what I do?' I said yes, and he helped me write and work on my sets. One night, Joe told me he was doing a headlining show for Scott at the Mandarin Yen and asked me if I would like to emcee for him. I said yes, and that's how Scott first saw me."

Jackson had Minjares vouch for him, which allowed him to cut the proverbial line to the Comedy Gallery stage. From there, he quickly became a Hansen regular. "Scott gave me a lot of work," he says. "I performed a lot at his Riverplace club. I remember he put me with George Wallace and let me open for him. That's was a blast, because he [Wallace] was so gracious and so nice. But for me, I got the bigger kick out of performing alongside guys like Alex Cole, Bill Bauer, and Jeff Gerbino. I'd heard so much about them, and it was a thrill for me."

Jackson says he and some of the other comics new to the scene were all very supportive of one another, as they worked to carve out their own niches. But Tom Hansen, who ran the open stages at River-place for many years, says it wasn't all love and kisses among the performers trying to claw their way through the Twin Cities comedy world. "We had a new group of comics, like John DeBoer, Colleen Kruse, and Jackie Kashian, who all got their start during that time,"

Hansen says. "It's funny because the comics were always buddies with each other—until they hit the stage. Then you'd see which comics didn't respect each other, because they would come talk to me while someone else was trying to perform. They were competitive."

Rick Carney echoes Tom's recollection, saying he felt that strong competitive spirit. "People on the scene got along," Carney remembers. "But I had friends who were big-time musicians in town, and the communities just weren't the same. Musicians were all friends, whereas in comedy there was definitely a hierarchy and cliques. I think a lot of that came from people, myself included, who had low self-esteem and just weren't confident in themselves. I remember we'd be watching closely whenever someone new would show up on the scene. Kind of like, 'Who is this guy?' and waiting to see if he's any good. Then we'd all breathe a sigh of relief when they weren't."

Despite this sense of competition, as well as the occasionally mixed feelings about Scott Hansen as a businessman, Tom Hansen says that maintaining a level of camaraderie among the performers was something his brother took very seriously. "Scott used to get all the comics who performed at all his different rooms together one night a week," he recalls. "He'd host a big family-style meal or have everyone go out together for drinks. That was really important to him."

Another new comic who started around this time was Fancy Ray McCloney. With his over-the-top Little Richard–inspired look, his fast tongue, and a showmanship unmatched by any type of performer in the Twin Cities—save maybe for Prince—McCloney was a personality one couldn't help but take notice of. He was a tireless self-promoter and worked hard to create his own opportunities for work, including in commercials and even his own public-access television show.

McCloney was working the open stage at the Comedy Gallery room inside Williams Pub in Uptown one night when he caught Hansen's eye. "I had been doing Pepitos on Sunday nights and just lighting the place on fire," McCloney recalls. "So I already had a strong reputation when I did the open stage at the Comedy Gallery in Uptown. One night, Scott came in to scout new acts for his regular rooms. He ended up taking me and Dwight York, and we got moved up to the next level."

Almost immediately, McCloney became a crowd favorite, and he got work opening for comics like Chris Rock (who McCloney says was very standoffish at this point in his career), Tommy Chong, and others. "I learned a lot watching those acts, but I also learned so much from the class of comedians I was coming up with at that point," McCloney remembers. "Comedy Gallery was definitely my main club."

While Riverplace continued as a roaring success, opening the new club in Galtier Plaza was an even bigger step for Hansen. The 350-seat club was his largest venue to date and allowed him to bring in acts he otherwise might have lost out on to cities with larger comedy spaces.

"It's a big step forward for entertainment in Downtown St. Paul," said Dick Zehring, the executive vice president of Zaidan Holdings, the company that owned and operated Galtier Plaza, during an interview with St. Paul's *Skyway News* in advance of the opening. "People have said for years that they wanted to find more to do in downtown at night."

Even with the extravagant new space and the fever pitch that stand-up comedy had achieved around town, Hansen was concerned that his Riverplace location, which was pulling in about forty percent of its audience from St. Paul and western Wisconsin, might lose customers to the St. Paul location, potentially leading to a thinning of crowds at both venues. He knew he needed something special to kick things off, something people hadn't seen before. It was time to get the band back together.

A comedy reunion was planned to celebrate the grand opening of the Galtier Plaza Comedy Gallery in October 1990, with Hansen, Bauer, Gerbino, and Cole coming together for the first time since their Mickey Finn's days to perform on the same stage, on the same night. The media ate it up. More than a decade after they first worked together in the noisy union bar in Minneapolis, four of the five originals were making front-page headlines once again: "Fab Four Make Comedy Reunion."

The opening show was an enormous success. It was followed later that month with big headliners like Pam Stone, who had become a TV sensation for her starring role on the sitcom *Coach*, and Carl

Wolfson, who was a staple of televised stand-up showcases like *Comic Strip Live* and *An Evening at the Improv*. Other major acts like George Wallace and Paula Poundstone were soon packing the club, while up-and-comers in Hansen's farm system of local comedians provided new blood and new shows at the Galtier Plaza venue and his other rooms around town.

Alex Cole, Bill Bauer, Scott Hansen, and Jeff Gerbino appeared on the cover of the Funny Paper *to celebrate the grand opening of Scott Hansen's Comedy Gallery at Galtier Plaza.*

One of the new, and very young, faces was that of Josh Weinstein. A St. Louis Park native, Weinstein might be the youngest comedian to ever grace the Comedy Gallery stages, getting his start at the age of fifteen. "It was very strange," remembers Weinstein. "I never talked about my age onstage, but I was a very diligent joke writer, and the other comedians saw that, so it kind of became irrelevant very quickly. People treated me like a peer, and I ate that up. By the time I was sixteen, I was doing a set almost every night."

After cutting his teeth as a regular at the HaHa Club as something of a protégé of Joel Hodgson, the comedy wunderkind made his way to the massive Riverplace location, where he met Hansen. "He was intimidating at first, certainly, because you knew he was the don of local comedy," Weinstein says of Hansen. "I just got into his system of doing open stage, seating people, emceeing, and featuring. Once he saw that I was a legit comic who wrote new jokes, he was happy to give me stage time. He was very supportive of me and gave me a lot of work at that club those first few years."

Weinstein was part of Hansen's new team of regulars, and he reaped the benefits of being able to open for established comics like Larry Miller and Bill Hicks, as well as rising stars like Dana Gould. But the night that stands out most is when Weinstein shared the stage with arguably the most famous name in stand-up comedy. "I opened for Henny Youngman one night at the St. Paul club," Weinstein says.

A comedy legend, Youngman was known as the "King of One-Liners," writing such iconic quips as, "Take my wife . . . please!"—a joke that has somehow survived generations. Youngman was well into his eighties by the time he performed at the Comedy Gallery, but he was still a massive draw. "He made a point to come in and watch my act, which I thought was very cool," Weinstein recalls. "Then he made me stand by the stage during his set in case he had to go to the bathroom. I was terrified because I had no idea what I was supposed to do if he had to go. Was it my job to take him to the bathroom? Was I supposed to fill time onstage? Fortunately he didn't have to go, so I never found out."

Having worked in the business for more than a decade by this point, Hansen had mastered the live comedy experience, and he seemed to have a Midas touch locally. But with his big Galtier Plaza club off and running, Hansen began to think even bigger. "Once I had the clubs going, I thought I had another product in me. I thought I had a television show," Hansen remembers. "I went to all the local TV stations and pitched them this thirty-minute show that would have cost them almost nothing to make. KARE 11 was very conservative at the time, so they shot me down. KSTP didn't quite have the reach—although we would go on to do some original programming with them later on. WCCO had no interest. But Channel 9 [KMSP] jumped on board."

After bouncing around as a Twin Cities affiliate of different national broadcast networks, KMSP had recently ended its relationship with the Fox network and become an independent station. It needed to find new and unique programming, preferably on the cheap. Hansen's proposal checked all the boxes.

Hansen had already done much of the legwork, and his large new club offered ample space for multiple camera angles and equipment, allowing for a truly professional production. Soon, *Comedy Gallery Live* hit the airwaves.

"We would do [live] shows out of both clubs on Sunday afternoons," Hansen explains. "And part of the contract for the headliners was that they had to do an afternoon show that could be used for a TV segment."

"If you're going to do a TV show, of course you're going to want the best," says McCloney, who was a two-time guest on the show.

The opportunity for TV time, albeit local, was an easy sell to national headliners coming to town. But the real value came for the local comics. From Kristin Andersen and Phyllis Wright to Alex Jackson and Ken Bradley, comedians who had developed a following in the clubs now had a platform for greater exposure to become household names. The show would in turn bring new fans into the clubs to see the real thing.

Jackson used *Comedy Gallery Live* as an opportunity to show off not only his stand-up skills but his acting chops. "We'd do stand-up, but then there would also be these little skits in between," he recalls. "We did one called 'drag racing.' It was literally just us in drag, racing. It was a blast to do, and for me, it was a way to get visibility to hopefully make the move out to Los Angeles."

With Hansen playing the role of host and ringmaster for each show, *Comedy Gallery Live* introduced audiences to a variety of performers doing a handful of their best bits. What Hansen didn't realize was that the reach was much larger than he had anticipated.

"It turned out that Channel 9 was the local Minneapolis news channel for all the cable networks from here to Montana," he says. "So our little 10:30 Friday night comedy show was in every market that didn't have broadcast news in their area. We were in Missoula, Montana, up into Canada, and over into Wisconsin. The craziest thing is that our show beat Letterman and *The Tonight Show* in the ratings [in those markets] every Friday."

This success led Hansen to book more clubs in states beyond Minnesota under the "Scott Hansen's Comedy Gallery" moniker. He also struck deals to film live television specials through his broadcast partner, booking shows in large theaters with thousands of people in attendance. "We did a Halloween live special, and an April Fools' Day special. Just really big shows," he recalls.

While Hansen would spread the wealth and feature acts who were regulars of his Comedy Gallery lineups, it was Jeff Gerbino, Alex Cole, Bill Bauer, and Hansen himself whose names consistently found their way onto those TV programs—a fact that did not sit well with some other comics in town. Still, Hansen says the decisions were based less on friendship or favoritism and more on a need to provide reliably strong content. "I needed good acts," Hansen says plainly. "I knew that Alex, Bill, and Jeff are all good acts. So if I get a call from someone like Showtime or *Star Search*, or I'm putting together a lineup for our specials, I knew I needed to give people the best comics we had. And that was them." And himself.

Though he would headline his clubs only sparingly, Hansen was still a performer, and he prided himself on showcasing his talents for crowds as well as for his fellow performers—sometimes even at their expense. "One time we were at the Riverplace room," John Bush remembers, "and it was an emcee, then me, and then the headliner, and

Press release for Comedy Gallery Live! *April Fools' special on KMSP-TV, which featured top local comedians as well as national acts like Paul Rodriguez*

Scott decided he was going to do a guest set in front of me. So Scott comes up to me after he's done, and I think he's joking, but he looks at me and goes, 'Follow that, fucker.' I'm like, 'Well this is *your* comedy club. Why would you want me to do badly at your club? Why would you burn me out of the stage at your club?' It was just very Scott."

Whether he was joking or not, Hansen's competitive spirit, mixed with his propensity to throw his proverbial weight around with other performers, didn't go away, regardless of how successful his clubs were. "The thing with Scott was that he was a comedian, and his ego played a part in how he behaved," says Weinstein. "There were times when he was very clearly going up in front of people to cause problems for them."

Weinstein says he believes part of Hansen's motivation was to puff out his chest and show national headliners who came to perform that he was on their level. "He built his act for that room and that crowd specifically," Weinstein continues. "You couldn't do his same set in Texas. So when big names came to town, I think he wanted to show them that he was one of them, and that he could be doing what they were if he had decided to."

Whether it was professional envy or strategic booking, Hansen's decision to put himself forward when a bigger name came to town was tough to argue with, since he was the one signing the checks. His choices regarding which other comics got stage time, however, soon became a hotly contested topic in the local comedy scene.

... **13** ...

Comedy Turmoil

Scott Hansen had solidified his place as the king of Minnesota comedy. As a performer, he was a legitimate headliner in the Twin Cities, and he was considered one of the smartest and funniest comedy writers anywhere. Fellow comedians took note of his knack for joke writing and structure, and many sought out Hansen to help them with their own acts.

"We booked Rob Schneider to come in and open for Dennis Miller in downtown Minneapolis at a theater show," Hansen recalls. "And Schneider was just eating it at these shows. He was a really sweet guy, and he was practically in tears talking to me one night. This was right after his 'Copier Guy' character came out on *Saturday Night Live*, and so the crowd would be sitting there waiting for him to do that bit the entire set. He'd bomb all the way until the end when he finally did it. Years earlier, I had seen Robin Williams perform right when *Mork & Mindy* was becoming a major hit, and when he came out he just buried Mork. He made the audience sick of hearing 'nanu nanu.' He would just do it for like fifteen minutes straight, so then the crowd didn't have to wait for it anymore. So Rob and I spent a whole week together restructuring his show. I got him to come out blasting Copier Guy in the beginning, then call it back at the end. A couple of days later he calls me from Milwaukee and says, 'Guess who's getting pissed at me?' and I said, 'Probably the headliner.' Because he was just killing every show."

Rob Schneider performing at Scott Hansen's Comedy Gallery at Riverplace. (Courtesy of Scott Hansen)

Tom Arnold, who had moved to Los Angeles to be a writer for his wife's sitcom, *Roseanne*, was another who sang Hansen's praises. Arnold called Hansen "a damn good comedy writer" and often inquired about Hansen joining him on his writing staff.

Meanwhile, Hansen continued to perform locally in his own clubs, regularly headlining while serving as an occasional host when a major name would come to town. "I was helping local promoter Sue McLean book comedy shows at the Guthrie Theater," he recalls. "So she booked Jerry Seinfeld and asked me to open. I was scheduled to perform maybe twenty minutes. I went out, did my time, and it went great. I came offstage, and there were still a lot of people waiting in line to get drinks from the bar, so Sue grabbed me and told me to go back out and do more until people were settled. So I went back out and did another twenty minutes. I walked off, and she ran up and told me she needed me to do more time. I went out and did maybe ten more minutes, and then finally I got the signal to wrap it up and bring out Seinfeld. As I'm walking off the stage, Seinfeld is just glaring at me. Not saying a word, just staring daggers. I was confused because I was doing what I was asked, and I had done a good job of warming up the crowd. Sue finds me in the lobby and says, 'Scott, I sold you out. Jerry was mad because he thought you were going to wear the crowd out and they'd be tired by the time he went on. I told him that you went over your time and I didn't know anything about it. I'm really sorry, but please don't say anything.' I kept that secret for her even though I had pissed off probably the biggest comedian of all time."

As well as his performing was going, it was nothing compared to the success he was enjoying as a promoter. At his peak, Hansen booked or operated more than forty comedy rooms, including the Comedy Gallery in Minneapolis, the sister location in St. Paul, and clubs stretching across Minnesota, such as one inside of a Howard Johnson's in Rochester, one inside of Grandma's Saloon in Duluth, and Belly Laughs at the Mandarin Yen restaurant in suburban Bloomington. Hansen also ran clubs in Arkansas, the Dakotas, Indiana, Iowa, Michigan, Missouri, Montana, Nebraska, Ohio, Wisconsin, Wyoming, and even Canada. This reach gave him incredible power not only when it came to bringing in new acts that were making names for themselves in markets outside the Twin Cities, but also in providing opportunities for local talents looking to make more money and gain more stage time by working in other cities.

"I would put people on the road and give them a full seven-day week of shows exclusively at our clubs," Hansen recalls. "Headliners were making around $1,200 to $1,500 per week, and middle acts were making about $700. No one else was doing that in comedy. In Minnesota especially, I was the biggest."

Hansen's brother Tom was also involved in booking these tours, which were known to the comics as the "Rambo Tours" and "Cheese Curd Tours." Recalls Tom: "They'd be a series of one-nighters that would run through the Dakotas and up into Canada. That was the Rambo Tour. The Cheese Curd Tours were the ones we'd run through Wisconsin. We had all sorts of names for them back then."

Rick Carney was a frequent part of these tours. A solid feature act, Carney got his start in 1988 and quickly hit the road. "The Rambo Tour ran from west to north," explains Carney. "You'd have a room added or dropped here and there, but for the most part that tour

VOL. 2, NO. 2, FEBRUARY 1987

FREE

TWIN CITIES

DIRECTORY

THE MONTHLY GUIDE TO WHAT WHEN & WHERE

COMEDY
BREAKS OUT
IN THE TWIN CITIES P. 6

BUNCHES OF BRUNCHES
WE'VE UNCOVERED
MORE THAN 60

GREAT ESCAPES
WINTER GETAWAYS
IN & OUT OF TOWN

Scott Hansen was the undisputed king of Twin Cities comedy in the late 1980s.

would hit St. Cloud, Grand Forks, Moorhead, and Fargo. The Cheese Curd Tour was the southeast: Rochester, Winona, La Crosse, and Eau Claire."

Although these tours provided comics with the opportunity to get on the road and make more money, they could also turn into a liability for the Hansen brothers as promoters. "I had a comedian named Frank Clawson who was doing the Rambo Tour," recalls Tom. "Frank was a very good comedian, and he decided to go out on this tour because it took him close to Rochester, where his father was getting treatment for cancer at Mayo. One day I get a call from a hotel in the middle of nowhere—I think it was Mayville, North Dakota—and they tell me that one of our comics has done some damage and we need to pay for it. This isn't the first time this had happened, so I say, 'okay, send me the bill.' Then I asked how much it was. The bill was $712. Back then, the comics are making like $1,000 to $1,500 a week, so that's a lot of money. I asked what happened, and they told me, 'Well, he pissed all over the bed.' And I said, 'Well that's not $700 worth of damage. What's a mattress cost? $100?' Then they told me he spread shit all over the walls, pissed all over the carpets, broke the toilet seat, knocked down the curtains in the shower. Just went completely rock and roll on the place. Now, I can't fire this guy or do anything else, because I can't get anyone else up to Bismarck, and I can't even reach him until he gets to Bismarck. I call my clients in Bismarck, tell them what happened, and ask if they can let me know if anything weird happens. The manager calls me back and says Frank was perfectly normal."

Clawson was traveling with Andy Jensen, his opener, on the tour, and Tom asked to be connected to Jensen's room to get the full story. "He gets on the phone and I ask, 'What's going on with Frank?' And he goes, 'Tom, I just had a ride with the devil. He was talking in tongues and doing all this weird stuff for the entire drive!' The shows went fantastic, though. So I bring Frank in on Monday to find out what happened. Turns out, he had started drinking that night to celebrate, because his father had been moved from the ICU to a general bed in the hospital. Well, Frank's a diabetic. So he was actually in a diabetic coma, walking around doing all this weird stuff. Unfortunately, I had to tell Frank he was never working for me again."

Another comedian who got quite a bit of road work from the Hansens was, unsurprisingly, Fancy Ray McCloney. "They would put me in the position to go in to a lot of clubs they were booking for the first time," McCloney recalls. "They'd have me come in and break in the rooms. Grand Forks, Fargo, Rochester, Mankato. They put me in a lot of places where I did really great. Now, at the time, Charlie Walker had been on the road and had some bad experiences as an African American. He got into some situations that were downright dangerous. And Charlie was 'safe.' So here I come with the full makeup and hair, and the most gorgeous clothes you've ever seen. I was even wearing lipstick for some shows. Scott and Tom were a little nervous to send me to some of those towns. Fortunately, I never had a problem. People would see my personality, and it would transcend race. Black room, white room—it didn't matter. Funny is funny and flamboyant is flamboyant. Some of those towns had different vibrations, but they were all great to me."

Even if road work was a fine opportunity for comics to make money and get exposure, it didn't always mean the work was good or the venues knew what they were doing. "Back then, people from all over the state would call Scott and say, 'We want to do comedy,'" says Carney. "And Scott would tell them that they need a microphone, and give them a price. So there wasn't necessarily a lot of vetting that went into it. I remember one night there were three of us on a tour, and our first stop is Hutchinson, Minnesota. They had never done comedy in this place before; we're the first ones to ever do it. So we get there, and there's a dart league going on. And the bar, they're telling us they can't turn off the dartboards, because they don't want to upset the regulars. Then on top of that, they set the stage up next to the bar, with the whole crowd off to our right. Plus it was about twenty below zero outside, and that was the day they buried a police officer who had been shot and killed. So we've got all that happening, and these bar owners would be like, 'And, go!' There was a lot of that kind of stuff on the road. There were really good places, and some really not good places."

There were clubs scattered throughout the Twin Cities that Hansen wasn't involved with, including Funny Bone and Raleigh's Rib Tickler in Minneapolis, but for the most part, anyone who wanted to be a successful comedian in Minnesota at that time had to work exclusively for Scott Hansen. Not everyone agreed with his tactics, though.

Ken Bradley got his start in comedy around 1985 after taking part in a comedy class taught by Joel Hodgson at the HaHa Club, the former Comedy Cabaret. After a few months of performing there, Bradley got the itch to move up in his comedy career. And that meant figuring out how to get in with Hansen. "I was getting gigs at the HaHa Club for maybe twenty-five or fifty dollars a weekend," Bradley recalls. "And I was doing maybe seven or ten minutes. I talked to a couple of other comedians, Rob Benton and Barry Fox, and told them, 'I need to get on the road.' Hansen was the one who booked all the road gigs, so they told me if I wanted to get more work, I had to go down and pray to the Big Buddha that was Scott."

Hansen was willing to give Bradley a shot, but he was going to have to work for it first. "These guys told me that you show up and meet Scott, and then offer to start seating people at his shows for free. Then, after a while, he'll let you get time on his open stages and maybe let you emcee."

Soon, Bradley was working almost full time for Hansen, though not just onstage. "I was working for him during the day, taking calls, seating, and then emceeing," he recalled. "I proved my loyalty, so Scott was letting me be a house emcee. Plus, he'd book me on the road on what we used to call Rambo Tours. It would be a bunch of one-nighters, but I'd make $800 in a week. That was big money back then. The best part was that I was being paid to do stand-up."

While Bradley is quick to give Hansen his due, he says the broader horizons came with a price. "He gave me a lot of opportunities, but in other ways he treated me like shit. But he treated a lot of people like shit. He would take his position and be abusive to you, and if you didn't take it, he wouldn't give you work. To me, it was pretty manipulative shit."

Another example of this manipulation, according to Bradley, was when Hansen asked him to perform at a benefit event in town, while leaving out a key detail. "Scott and I had very different political beliefs," Bradley recalls. "I didn't do any political humor or anything like that, but he knew I was more liberal and I knew he was much more conservative. So he asks me if I can help him out and go do a benefit show one weekend. I'm always happy to help, so I agree and head down there. What he didn't tell me was that it was a benefit for the Young Republicans. I took one look around and thought, 'I don't want to perform for these fuckers!' That was his way of digging at me a little."

Hansen had built a reputation, both good and bad, among the comedians in town. But it wasn't until a reporter named David Brauer decided to do a story about Hansen for the *Twin Cities Reader* that his influence became known to those who weren't on the inside of the scene. "David had talked to a ton of people, and he said that no one would talk to him [about Hansen]," Bradley remembers. "At that point I had a real fuck-the-man attitude, so I told David I'd talk to him."

One of the first questions Brauer had for Bradley was about the contracts Hansen was requiring comedians to sign before allowing them to perform at his clubs. "When the Funny Bone was here, he told comics, 'If you go there, you won't work for me,'" Bradley told Brauer. "At one point, Scott had the top four venues in town and was trying to make all comics sign exclusive contracts. It probably isn't legally binding, just a scare tactic for anyone who would fall for it."

The contracts in question gave Hansen a comedian's exclusive performance rights within a fifty-mile radius for twelve months, unless he personally approved a booking. Essentially, Hansen was monopolizing comics' Twin Cities bookings for an entire year. In exchange, Hansen offered benefits such as priority for lucrative private and corporate comedy events, though there were no guarantees.

"David asked me, 'So if you perform two nights in St. Cloud, you can't book anything else without his permission in the Twin Cities for the next year?'" Bradley says. "So I walked over to a drawer in the house and pulled out a stack of contracts that I hadn't signed. He asked me how I was able to get away without signing them. I told him that Tom Hansen likes me."

According to Bradley, Scott Hansen often had his brother Tom be the one to work with the comedians on getting contracts signed and returned. Whereas comedians were fairly evenly divided in their opinions of Scott, Tom was more universally liked among those in the scene.

"I remember one time Tom called me and told me they had a gig for me all lined up, and they just needed that contract back," Bradley says. "And I said, 'Tom, I really want to get you that contract. But I assume that when I give it to you, you're going to hand me back a guarantee that I'll have shows booked every night for the next 365 nights, right?' And he just laughed. He got it, and he let me skirt the system. He probably would have kept letting me do it too, but I had to be cocky and arrogant and flaunt what I was doing to David Brauer. After that, I was blackballed for a pretty significant amount of time."

Eventually, Brauer was able to get other comedians to agree to be interviewed for his story, though some would only participate under the condition of anonymity, out of fear of retribution. "You have to understand what kind of hold Scott Hansen has," said one of Hansen's employees in the article. "He thinks he's the only guy who can make his clubs work, so he treats his comics like absolute crap."

These gripes didn't go unheard by Hansen, though he insists he was merely protecting his business. "I would tell comics I could guarantee them they would get enough work if they chose to work with my clubs," he says. "But if they chose to work at another club, I couldn't use them in my clubs as often. It's just common sense. If someone saw you at the club down the street last week, how am I supposed to have you perform at my club the next week and expect anyone to care?"

Tom echoes his brother's stance on the contracts, defending the idea both as a fan and from a business standpoint. "The contracts stemmed from the fact that we had comics who would perform at one of our clubs one week, then be at a club down the street two weeks later," says Tom. "We'd spend a lot of money on advertising, and this other club wouldn't. But since we just put all this money into promoting this comic, they'd still get business from it. On top of that, we'd charge maybe ten or fifteen dollars, and these other clubs would be charging less. So people were seeing the same talent for a cheaper price. Finally, let's say they worked our club and got paid $800. They'd turn around and work this other club for $400. So if you're working the same amount for half the money down the street, why would we pay you double that? That's the only reason the contracts were done. The comics don't see it that way, but it's true. And honestly, we had more work to offer. You want ten weeks of work throughout the year? We can give that to you. If we didn't use that type of leverage to our advantage in a business capacity, it would have been a mistake."

In addition to Bradley and a few unnamed comedians, some of Hansen's longtime friends and collaborators openly criticized his methods in the *Twin Cities Reader*. Joel Hodgson, who once broke the Comedy Gallery attendance record and was a frequent headliner for Hansen early on, felt the club owner was developing a stranglehold on the local comedy scene. Once Hodgson had established his own star power, he chose not to sign a contract with Hansen and decided to stop performing at his clubs entirely. "I just feel like Scott's misused his resources, as far as the Minneapolis audience and its talent pool," Hodgson told Brauer.

Frank Conniff, who would go on to partner with Hodgson on *Mystery Science Theater 3000*, also shared his opinions about Hansen for the article, and he would suffer the consequences.

"Frank Conniff was working for Scott before I was," Bradley remembers. "People used to call us Scott's lackeys. It really pissed me off at the time, but they were right. There was me, and there was Frank, and before him there was someone else. I didn't like it, but it's how you got your foot in the door."

Conniff was interviewed for the piece on a Thursday, during a week in which he was booked to perform at the Comedy Gallery in St. Paul. On Saturday afternoon, Hansen called Conniff and told him to skip the early show that night, which happened to be when a national TV talent scout was attending the performance. Conniff was the only performer instructed not to show up, and a dozen other comics were still invited to perform. "He did it out of retribution," Conniff said. "It's the only logical explanation. Otherwise, he just wanted to deny me an opportunity."

When pressed on why he cut Conniff from the lineup that night, Hansen explained to Brauer that it wasn't a vendetta, but rather that the scout was looking for someone who could play a teenager, and Conniff, who was thirty-four years old at the time, just didn't fit the bill. That story is plausible, except for the fact that Jeff Gerbino performed that night, and Gerbino is three years older than Conniff.

Another former frequent Hansen collaborator, Jeff Cesario, defended his old Mickey Finn's colleague, in part. Cesario, who had graduated to full-blown headliner on the West Coast by this time, regularly came back to town to perform at Hansen's clubs, and he praised Hansen for his ability to line up media and generate buzz for comics. However, Cesario also spoke out against some of Hansen's borderline bullying tactics. "Stuff like making opening acts and middle acts sign something where they couldn't perform at other clubs, that's just bullshit," Cesario told Brauer. "Why should he care if some struggling comic is playing somewhere else? It's the headliners people come to see. The young comic will only build a following and bring you more business down the road."

As Bradley noted, comics who did choose to play ball with Hansen were given plenty of opportunities to perform outside of Minnesota at the other clubs Hansen managed. "I worked with some incredible comics, and that was a pretty good school for someone trying to make it in comedy," Bradley says. "I think that's how Scott looked at it too, which is why he could get away with not paying as much sometimes or being a total dick to people."

Some seasoned comics, however, argued that Hansen was doing these performers a disservice by putting them on the road too early, before they had time to develop their acts more fully. Hodgson was especially critical, claiming that Hansen was rushing some of his preferred comics on the road in order to fulfill his extensive road bookings. "By putting people on the road real early, they don't get a chance to really grow," Hodgson told Brauer. "You're not in a place like Minneapolis, where audiences are alert, and you end up doing a lot of easy humor."

Carney acknowledges that he could see the talent pool getting watered down, especially when it came to road work. "If I'm being honest, I'm probably a part of that watering down," he admits. "If there were fewer clubs and opportunities, I wouldn't have been included [in the tours]. But for me, the worst part were the road dogs [comedy slang for performers who did one-shot road gigs, without

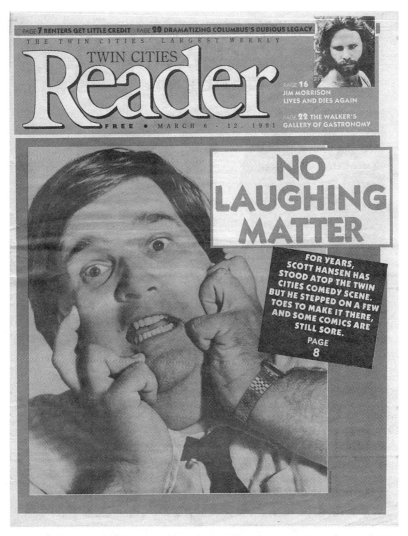

In March 1991, David Brauer's exposé on the turmoil within Scott Hansen's comedy empire was published in the Twin Cities Reader.

giving much attention to working on their jokes]. They would try out new jokes on you in the car, which were awful. Then they'd get up onstage that night and a joke would bomb, and you'd be thinking to yourself, 'That joke didn't even work in the car.'"

Lizz Winstead, who has become one of the most prominent national names to emerge from the Twin Cities comedy scene of that time, was a Comedy Gallery regular in the mid- to late eighties, and she sings Hansen's praises for helping her grow her own career. She defends him against the assertion that he played favorites. "He gave me a shitload of opportunities early on," she says today. "I don't think he booked comedians just because they were his friends. I think he became friends with comics to varying degrees, but no one got opportunities who didn't deserve them."

That said, in the *Twin Cities Reader* article, Winstead offered a similar perspective as Hodgson and Carney about whether some comics may have been given prominent roles by Hansen earlier in their careers than they should have. "Scott brought in really great national acts, really good people," she said. "But some of the local middles he used, you just had to wonder, why? He sent a lot of people on the road who came back with a lot of lowest common denominator comedy."

Many of the old-timers, meanwhile, stuck by Hansen's side. The other members of the original five—Louie Anderson, Alex Cole, Jeff Gerbino, and even Bill Bauer—all had cordial working relationships with Hansen and often performed at his clubs. By the late eighties, Cole was partnering with Hansen in booking comedians for road gigs. As both a longtime performer and a friend of Hansen's, he was quick to jump to his defense. According to Cole, the issue wasn't that Hansen was putting new comics on the road too soon, but rather that the national comedy boom had caused everyone to accelerate the process of putting new talent in front of crowds. "The comedy boom brought such an explosion that you had to book acts that had been doing comedy for twenty minutes," Cole told Brauer.

"The stink of the road," as it is often referred to by comedy purists, means using easy, lowbrow humor to get cheap laughs instead of focusing on writing or growing as a performer. This is something that many comics, like Conniff, said wasn't just evident in the comics Hansen booked but in Hansen's own performances as well. "The thing about Scott is he's very talented, but he stopped growing as a comic when he started getting busier," Conniff told Brauer. "He was a great crowd-rap comic; he could talk with an audience and come up with things. Eventually, he just started doing jokes like, 'Hey, I'll fall on you.'"

Cesario agreed with Conniff's assessment of Hansen as a performer, wondering why his old friend didn't make more of an effort to push himself comedically. "It was a big deal for him to do fifteen minutes before me or Louie when we came to town," Cesario said. "You want to say, 'Scott, you can do better!'"

To his credit, Hansen wasn't blind to the challenges of running the business side of comedy while trying to keep himself sharp as a performer. "I've got two of the best clubs in the country and I can't even use them the way I would like to as a comic," he told the *Reader*, defending himself against the piercing words of his fellow comics. "I'm not working my rooms when I could be a middle every week in one of my clubs. Of all the comics in town, when I headline I set attendance records, but I don't walk into those rooms and play them every week. There's a lot of things that comics don't know about."

While some were quick to bash Hansen and others stayed tight-lipped for fear of retribution, others, like his old friend Tom Arnold, jumped to his defense. "If it wasn't for Scott there wouldn't be local comedy in Minneapolis," Arnold said. "He stuck with it, and put it all together as a business. He took all the risks. He's the reason that fifty guys made it, because he gave them so much stage time. Without him, all you'd see in the good clubs would be out-of-towners booking other out-of-towners."

Similarly, comedian Alex Jackson says that, although he butted heads with Hansen on occasion, he believes the vitriol spewed by other comics was the result of their own passive-aggressive nature and inability to communicate with Hansen. "Scott only said to me one time, 'If you work for this person, then you can't work for me,'" Jackson recalls. "And I wasn't a starving artist or anything. I had a full-time job. So I told him, 'Look, I won't work for another person's room in a place where you have a room. That's fair. But if you don't have something there, and someone wants to book me, I'm going to work. No one owns me.' And we butted heads. His brother Tom called me up, and we butted heads too. But then we got over it. I think sometimes you need to have that kind of discussion to know where each other's boundaries are. Sure, I heard about the rifts and

I knew people who didn't like him, but I always found him to be fair, and if we had a disagreement, we'd talk it out."

Fancy Ray was another who chose to simply work out these issues with Hansen. "I knew about the politics, and it very much took place. But I transcended all of that," McCloney says. "I was always a person who said, 'I've got to eat. I got to go where the money is.' Sometimes you needed to be strategic about turning down work from certain promoters or certain clubs, but for whatever reason I got a pass. I think Scott saw that my personality was bigger than the agent."

Regardless of the differences of opinion over Hansen's treatment of the comics, most performers agree that Hansen helped more of them than he hurt. And as for those he may have hurt, Bradley contends that it was rooted in some personal insecurities on Hansen's part. "He's got his own demons he's burying," Bradley says. "I remember once that Seinfeld was in town, and I was backstage with him before the show. I was there because I was Scott's lackey, Scott was there, Joel Hodgson was there because he and Seinfeld were friends and he was his opener, and I think there were a few others. We're all sitting there reading newspapers before the show, trying to come up with new stuff we can talk about, and Scott says, 'Hey, Jerry. After the show, what do you say we all go out to Market Bar-B-Que and get something to eat?' And Jerry lowers his newspaper and says, 'Scott, you've eaten.' And we all bury our faces in the newspapers because we don't want Scott to kill us. It was a funny line by Seinfeld, but in that moment I could feel Scott's embarrassment and sadness. I drove home with him after the show, and I could feel the shame. I really think that's where some of Scott's viciousness came from."

Adds Carney, "We were all self-conscious back then, and had our own issues. That included Scott. But he was the guy who everybody loved and hated, since he was the power guy. I think keeping that power was very important to him. It's funny because comics would sit down and complain about him to the other comics, and then as soon as he walked in it would be smiles and waves. I remember one time a comic came up to me and another comic named Mike Nelson before the open stage at Riverplace. He goes, 'Man, how about this stuff in

South Africa? The whole apartheid thing? That's just really screwed up.' Then he takes a pause and says, 'Do you guys think Scott likes my act?' So that was a lot of how people would interact with Scott back then."

After the Brauer story was published, the divide within the comedy community became even deeper. According to Bradley, though, it impacted the competing venues more than it did the performers. "Scott had such a big handprint in the comedy scene that if one of the clubs he didn't run was bringing someone to town, he'd call and offer them more money to perform at his place, on the condition they didn't perform with his competition," he recalls. "But for comedians, he did give a lot of opportunities. He did a ton for me, letting me work with people like Bill Maher and Ellen DeGeneres. I credit him for that entirely. And after the article came out, I felt like kind of a punk for throwing that all back in his face."

Eventually, Bradley and Hansen would reconcile, as Hansen was known as someone who didn't hold grudges. But the struggles taking place among the comics was nothing compared to the struggles happening within some of the comics themselves.

14

Vices

Even as the comedy business was booming, with that success came plenty of demons. Bill Bauer was one comic who had a reputation on the scene for issues with substance abuse and occasionally letting the partying go too far, but there were many others who struggled with vices during the formative years of comedy in the Twin Cities.

"One of my early disenchantments in show business was when I opened for Danny Bonaduce [of *Partridge Family* fame] at the Comedy Gallery Riverplace," recalls John Bush. "At the end of his set, he says, 'I've been sober for two years,' and the whole crowd goes nuts for him. The show ends, and we go into the back bar, and he goes, 'Hey, let's do some shots!' That's when I learned that some parts of comedy are all bullshit."

Tom Hansen had become a much bigger part of his brother Scott's businesses around the time they opened the Riverplace club. In addition to managing some of the smaller rooms his brother ran, Tom would help to wrangle some of the high-profile comedians Scott brought to town. That, he says, was anything but a normal job.

He recalls, "Tom Arnold would hand me an eightball of cocaine before he got onstage and have me go cut lines for him on the bathroom counter. Then he'd pretend to follow a woman to the bathroom, do those lines, and get back up onstage." Hansen adds that Arnold was the person who introduced him to cocaine for the first time, "and I fell in love with it."

Arnold has long been open about his struggles with drugs and alcohol, and Hansen often had a front-row seat. "Tom was working a show for me in St. Cloud at a bar called Charlie's," he remembers. "And his nose starts bleeding from doing so much coke. So an audience member thought it would be funny to throw a tampon onstage. Tom took it, put it up his nose, and did the last fifteen minutes of his set. When that bar closed, Tom Arnold's dried blood was still on the stage."

Tom Hansen also found himself "working" some unusual hours in his role as well. "Drew Carey would come to town to perform at Riverplace, and he would have me take him out to the strip clubs every night after he was done." Tom laughs, "Every single time he'd come to town. We got to be kind of buddies, and the man loved strip clubs. It's funny because if you only know him from TV you'd think he was so wholesome, but his onstage act was 'fuck-fuck-fuck-fuck' everything. But he was one of the funniest guys I worked with and just a very nice person."

Carey wasn't the only performer who enjoyed sampling the adult nightlife the Twin Cities had to offer. "Charles Fleischer performed at Riverplace. If you ever saw the movie *Who Framed Roger Rabbit?*, he was the voice of Roger Rabbit." Tom continues, "He would want me to bring him to the strip clubs too. And he'd get in there and be doing the Roger Rabbit voice, so strippers were always circling him. They loved it."

As for the original five, they had their own struggles. One Hansen employee, who asked to remain nameless (we'll call him Doug), spent years watching the group blaze a trail of pain and self-destruction when they were offstage. "I used to tell people that I was an underpaid babysitter. And I was," Doug says. "When you look at the broad spectrum of comedians, probably three-quarters of them had some kind of issue. Not just drugs or alcohol, either."

Scott Hansen, for his part, was not known to get out of control when it came to drugs or alcohol, but according to Doug, he found another way to fill the void. "Scott's vice is food," he says. "He's had countless people try to talk to him about losing weight. His attitude was always, 'If you don't like me how I am, then you can leave.' It was a really unhealthy lifestyle."

Some of that lifestyle, Doug describes, was less about Hansen and more about the nature of the comedy business. "It wasn't all Scott's fault. Most comedians back then weren't living a healthy lifestyle. They would get up at noon, and that's about when Scott would get up. Except Scott would go to McDonald's on the way to the office. Then he'd get to the office and everyone was eating lunch, so he'd partake in lunch. Then the shows aren't until 7 or 8 PM every night, so we'd all go eat dinner. Then by the time we were done with the shows, it would be 1 AM, and Scott would go home and cook himself what he considered his next dinner."

While Hansen made it a point to not let his weight dictate his act, it was something he had at his disposal for an easy punch line. But to Doug, it wasn't anything to laugh about. "He'd do jokes onstage where he'd say, 'I'll fall on you. And you'll get sucked up in the pressure,' or something like that. People would laugh, but I didn't find it funny. I never laughed. I think deep down inside a lot of that had to hurt. And I know people joked about it, but I think it was something he was really battling."

Alex Cole was another who succumbed to the vices of the 1980s comedy and entertainment world. Few can knock Cole's abilities onstage or his work ethic as a comic, but the stories of his partying and drug use in the later part of the decade are equally undeniable. "Alex used to pretend like he was following someone to the bathroom [as part of a joke] when he was performing, and then do cocaine and get back onstage," says Tom Hansen. "He told me once he spent $40,000 in a year on cocaine. That's a lot of money by today's standards, but he did this back in like 1988."

Cole's drug use was fairly well known, but the types of situations he'd get himself into once he was drunk or high were nearly unbelievable. "Alex did some strange stuff," Hansen says with a laugh. "One night he let a blind girl drive his car home. I think she was legally blind. He was so drunk and high, and this girl was also drunk, but she wanted to drive him home, so he let her. He gave her directions and helped her, but she did it."

Doug echoes those sentiments regarding Cole's hard-partying ways. "Alex loved cocaine. He couldn't get enough," he says. "At one point, Scott had enough and said he wouldn't book him anymore. But Alex still had his college tour stuff. I know he eventually burned a bridge with a college, which finally made him decide he needed to clean up."

In Cole's case, Scott Hansen had to provide some tough love. But for others, he went above and beyond in helping them battle their addictions. "Scott paid to put at least five comics through rehab," Doug recalls.

Tom Hansen recalls that a big reason for his brother's commitment to helping his fellow comics in this way stems from his witnessing the tragedy that can result. "Ron Douglas was one of the funniest comedians in the Twin Cities. He was really good friends with Scott," Hansen explains. "He moved out to LA, but he would stay at Scott's house when he came back to perform. Ron passed away from being an alcoholic. That's why Scott tried to help others. He didn't want to see that happen to anyone else."

Among those whom Hansen helped put through treatment were Chris Raine and Tom Arnold. Tom Hansen says his motivations were completely earnest. "He never really talked about it," Hansen says. "He just paid the money, and they went to treatment, and that was it. Scott was very respectful of their privacy."

The number of people who passed away during this era in comedy is sadly extensive, many of them lost to their own vices. "I dug through the list of all the people we started with who have passed away," says Cole. "Ron Douglas drank himself to death, then there was Warner Jackson, Holly Henson, Roman Dicaire, Bruce Murray. Dan Bradley ended up killing himself in Denver. Barry Fox, Chris Raine, Gary Johnson, Dave Young, and of course Bill Bauer. That's a pretty long list."

Narratives of the 1980s Twin Cities comedy scene are equal parts success story of those who went on to bigger and better things and cautionary tale of the pitfalls of that world and the destruction it left in its wake. Tom Hansen says that the act of getting onstage as a comic is as much motivated by the drive for that success as it is a recipe for, and sign of, illness. "The simple fact that somebody wants to be onstage like that typically means they have an issue," Tom Hansen says. "To even want to take that kind of criticism, you have to have issues. Look at it like this: If you're in a band and you have a bad show, you can say that the drummer was off, or you were playing Top 40 that wasn't even your music. If you're a comic, it's just you up there. It's your jokes, your timing. I really respect anyone who is willing to get up there like that."

··· **15** ···

A Woman's Place Is in the Spotlight

In the early days of stand-up, there was no debating the fact that it was a man's world. Locally, it was rare to see a woman take the stage at Mickey Finn's or any of the bars that took an early chance on comedy. Talk to any woman in stand-up, past or present, and she'll likely have numerous stories of sexism, harassment, and the general "boy's club" mentality that permeated the scene.

While certainly not perfect or without exception, Minnesota was generally ahead of the curve when it came to providing female comedians with a platform to showcase their talents and improve at their craft. Dudley Riggs was one of the first to actively promote female-driven stand-up shows. And it originated with Susan Vass.

Vass got her start as a joke writer, and she would submit ideas to Louie Anderson, who was a regular in Riggs's Minneapolis Comedy All-Stars. Impressed with her work, Anderson encouraged Vass to perform the jokes herself. That was the birth of the all-female stand-up showcase "What's So Funny About Being Female?" At this monthly event at the Experimental Theater Company (ETC), Vass would lead a group of female comedians who were finding their voices in a predominately male industry.

Similarly, across town, Scott Hansen was providing opportunities for comics—male or female—to gain stage time and build relationships with national headliners coming through town. It didn't matter to Hansen the sex, race, or style of the comic—he just wanted people who were funny. Still, it wasn't easy being a woman in a room full of

Lily Tomlin (center) makes a visit to Dudley Riggs's ETC Theater for "What's So Funny About Being Female?" Directly behind Tomlin is Karen Pickering, and to Tomlin's left is Priscilla Nelson. (Courtesy of Priscilla Nelson)

guys, and Hansen ultimately took things one step further: he opened the female-only "Scott Hansen's Rib Tickler Women's Comedy Nightclub," hosting female headliners, emcees, and feature acts. Operating out of a barbecue place on North First Street in Minneapolis, the club itself was short-lived, but Hansen's dedication to helping female comics carve a path continued.

Despite the opportunities, hormones and backstabbing were prevalent, and female comedians were often caught in the cross fire. Rick Carney recalls how hard it was for Bridget Nelson, who would go on to be an integral part of the *Mystery Science Theater 3000* gang along with her husband, Mike. "The male comics wouldn't leave her alone," says Carney, who was close with both Bridget and Mike in their Comedy Gallery days. "She'd have the male comics hanging on her, asking her out. They all hated Mike because she was dating him. It was nonstop."

Challenges aside, the roster of female comics who traveled from all over the country to perform in Minnesota, from Roseanne Barr to Ellen DeGeneres, was impressive. But the local women of Twin Cities comedy, the homegrown talents who muscled their way into the rooms and commanded the microphones, truly paved the way for the next generations and established their own voices that continue to shape stand-up today.

Lizz Winstead

Lizz Winstead killed her first time onstage (back then, it was just "Liz," with one "z"). It was December 1983 at Dudley Riggs's ETC. At the urging of her friends, Winstead stepped onstage during the club's Sunday open mic night following a performance of the Minneapolis Comedy All-Stars.

Mike Gandolfi, Lizz Winstead, Paul Dillery, and Scott Hansen. (Courtesy of Scott Hansen)

"I wasn't particularly interested in stand-up," Winstead recalls. "I mean, I loved George Carlin. He was kind of an inspiration for me, and I really enjoyed Letterman's morning show. But I was a student studying history at the University of Minnesota. Being a comedian wasn't my dream or something I would have even thought about."

But Winstead wasn't about to back down from a dare. She went up on the stage that night and instantly felt the magic. "I tried it, and I was hooked," she says. "I come from a big family, and all I could think was, 'This is so great to have people sitting there and not talking while I'm talking.'"

Her jokes were well received that night, and Winstead's confidence was through the roof. It wouldn't last. "Adrenaline gets you through your first time," she explains. "Plus the emcee usually lets everyone know it's your first time, so the crowd is on your side. I got some laughs with my stupid jokes, and I decided to go back the next Sunday. I totally bombed. I had so much false confidence. So I decided to go back again the next week, and I was marginal, so I figured maybe it was worth trying some more."

Winstead continued to get up onstage at the ETC, and she also started going around town in search of stage time at other venues in the Twin Cities' budding comedy scene. "I remember going down to do open mic at the Comedy Cabaret quite a bit, and I even did that crazy club in Northeast called Mickey Finn's maybe once or twice right toward the end. But for the most part it was either the Comedy Cabaret or Dudley Riggs."

As one of the owners of the Comedy Cabaret at the time, Stephanie Hodge had the opportunity to see Winstead find her voice early on. "I remember watching Lizz and thinking that she was really funny," she recalls. "And I remember saying to someone, 'God, if she wrote stuff, can you imagine?' It always hit me the way she told jokes that if she wrote her stuff all out it would be really interesting to read too."

Around that time, the split between the Comedy Cabaret partners created a rift not only among the club promoters but among the comics themselves. "Club owners weren't really getting along and playing nice with each other," Winstead recalls, "and I somehow ended up in the Comedy Gallery camp with Scott Hansen."

Hansen recognized Winstead's talent and almost immediately began scheduling her to host the Comedy Gallery's open mic night. He also played a role in helping to establish her as a bona fide headliner locally. "Scott was really instrumental in getting me exposure and bringing me out to the one-nighters in those smaller satellite towns like Alexandria, Grand Forks, Minot, Duluth, Mankato. Just traveling to some bar and getting paid seventy-five dollars to do a set."

Winstead also began to form friendships with other local comics, including members of the original five. And thanks to Hansen, she got the opportunity to open for some of the biggest traveling acts to come through town. Winstead recalls, "Scott gave me the chance to open for Leno. I opened for Seinfeld. I remember when Roseanne was coming to town pretty regularly from Denver, he would let me perform with her. That opened a lot of doors for me."

Before long, the woman who had no interest in performing stand-up had reached a level where she was ready to headline the Comedy Gallery. She would become the first homegrown female comic to be a solo headliner at the club. "The first time I headlined, Louie Anderson flew in to open for me to make sure people would come and see me," she says.

"She was a rebel right from the beginning," says Anderson. "She was doing satire, and she had a point of view. She had one of the early points of view that was so strong. She was kind, but she wasn't a pushover."

Winstead admits that part of the reason she was able to excel as a performer was the double standard that female comics experienced from both club owners and male comics. "When you were a woman doing comedy, you weren't viewed as a threat to the guys," Winstead says. "Clubs wouldn't book more than one woman on a show, unless it was one of these all-women shows, which always felt like a dumb way to book women. But still, male comics weren't really afraid of you taking their spot, so they were a little more welcoming to me."

Though the Minneapolis stand-up scene was relatively progressive in its attitude toward women performers, Winstead is quick to point out that other markets weren't so forward-thinking. "I'd do road gigs in the Dakotas or even in some of the more rural parts of the state, and as soon as the crowd would see a woman onstage they'd kind of roll their eyes like they were getting ripped off," she recalls. "So then the promoters would just be like, 'Let's sandwich her in between a couple of men. That should work.'"

Sexist? Definitely. Small-minded? Without question. But in the end, those attitudes allowed Winstead to have the last laugh. "No one wanted to open their show with a woman," she says. "They were afraid it might set the wrong tone. So I really wasn't someone who had to emcee very long. I moved right up to middle act and got more stage time and made more money. And it wasn't because I was that good; it was because these guys were scared that a woman opening would kill the rest of their show."

In addition to regular spots at Hansen's various comedy rooms, Winstead found other opportunities to get onstage, including a gig as the emcee for First Avenue's weekly dance contest, as well as a weird and wonderful Tuesday night show in the 7th Street Entry alongside Tom Arnold and his Goldfish Review. For a brief time in the early eighties, she and Arnold cohosted a Wednesday-night comedy series, Comedicus Spasticus, in the Entry.

As she advanced her own career, Winstead forged relationships with other women comics on the scene and helped pave the way for new female performers to get a fair shake. "I felt really welcome," Winstead remembers. "Susan Vass was the biggest woman performing in town at the time, and we got along—Karen Pickering, Stephanie Hodge, Phyllis Wright. There were some really funny women, and we all really wanted to help each other. There was a lot of male energy back then, and as a woman your life experience is different. For a while, there was this idea in comedy, not just locally but everywhere, that women should only do material about things that are universal. We were told not to talk about our experience as a woman, because it needed to be something everyone could enjoy. Meanwhile I'm sitting there thinking, 'I just had to listen to you talk about your male experience, and we're all supposed to enjoy that.' And I tried. I tried just doing observational stuff for a while, but then I just said fuck it because it felt disingenuous. I don't have another lens besides being a woman."

Winstead also served as something of a mentor and teacher for some of her female counterparts, like Karen Pickering. "I was in a women's show with her at the Comedy Gallery, and she would help me craft my jokes," recalls Pickering. "She had just graduated college maybe two years earlier, and was getting a lot of good work. The audiences loved her and hated her while they laughed. She was always able to speak her politics and get the laugh. Lizz was absolutely brilliant."

Around 1987, Winstead left Minnesota for the West Coast. She began performing in San Francisco with the help of several comics she had connected with during her time in the Twin Cities. "The San Francisco comics would stay at my apartment when they'd come to town to work the Comedy Gallery," she says. "It was so great because it was all these really strong headliners who didn't have a draw yet, and I had the chance to become friends with them, and then they helped me when I moved out west."

Over time, Winstead established herself as one of the funniest, smartest, and most daring comedians anywhere. She helped create *The Daily Show*, one of the most iconic and successful political comedy shows of all time. But even now, nearly forty years after she got onstage for the first time, Winstead still beams about the comedy town where she got her start.

"Minneapolis audiences were just the best audiences. They were great," she says. "They gave you the freedom to work out your shit, and they would judge you on a joke-by-joke basis. If they didn't like something, they wouldn't just cancel you altogether. It was really welcoming and really smart and just felt like a place where everyone was in it together."

Priscilla Nelson

Like many others in the early stand-up comedy boom, Priscilla Nelson got the itch to try comedy by hanging around comedians.

Working in the box office of Dudley Riggs's ETC, she became friends with the crew of the Minneapolis Comedy All-Stars. "All of those guys were really nice and very inspiring to me. Especially Louie," she recalls. "We'd all go out to dinner on Sundays after the

The "What's So Funny About Being Female?" shows provided a big boost for Priscilla Nelson's comedy career. Shown here is the poster for the 1986 performance.

show, and I got the chance to become close with Louie. He was a comedy genius, and he inspired me to try an open stage of my own."

With a knack for joke writing, it didn't take much for Nelson to whip up a short set to bring onstage. "It was 1982, and I went to the Comedy Cabaret and asked Scott Novotny and Stephanie Hodge if I could try it. I got up and did five minutes of comedy, and I was very funny. Then I wasn't funny for about two years after that."

While she may not have been a comedy prodigy, Nelson kept working on developing her stage persona, primarily at the ETC and Comedy Cabaret. Then she caught a break. "Susan Vass started producing her 'What's So Funny About Being Female?' show and asked me to be a part of it," Nelson recalls. "It was such a big leg up in terms of giving me stage time and helping me to connect what I thought was funny to the right audience."

Karen Pickering met Nelson during an open mic night at the ETC and was instantly drawn to her. "She was a feminist without anyone really knowing it," says Pickering. "Her material took the antics of men, [the] Victoria's Secret catalog, and what she saw in society and made it so damn funny. You didn't even know how much you were learning until the next day, when you were telling the joke at work."

After about four months of performances, Nelson made the move across town to work for Scott Hansen at the Comedy Gallery. "Scott started booking me quite a bit and booked me for a lot of gigs all over the Midwest," she says. "It was a lot of fun. I got to travel a lot, had some really good shows, had some really horrible shows, and made some great friends."

Similar to Winstead, Nelson had to endure plenty of sexism during her time on the road, especially outside of the Twin Cities. "I had a club owner in Rochester get mad at me when I showed up," she says. "He looked at me and goes, 'I didn't know they were going to send me a woman.' But then I ended up having a really good show, so he was much nicer to me after that. Still, I don't think I ever went to a club that hired two women for one show. It was still a very white male–dominated world."

In contrast to Winstead, however, Nelson's perception was that the women in comedy during this era were actually more competitive than their male counterparts. "I was pretty sheltered for a while, being in the 'What's So Funny' show. Everyone who came knew it was going to be an all-women show, and it was wildly popular. But once you got outside of that, there was a lot of competition among women comics. The market was so much narrower for us, because we knew clubs would only hire one female at most for certain shows, so those spots became much more coveted. The male comics would share information with each other about club owners and contacts, but we [female comics] kept it all to ourselves because the competition was so much greater. It was tough because the club owners tended to think that all women comics were the same. That we were all going to talk about the same women's things."

In the face of these challenges and limited opportunities, Nelson says the women who managed to stick around in comedy made it because of their talent. "There weren't a lot of women doing comedy back then, but the ones who were doing it were really good," she says.

By performing at Dudley Riggs and the Comedy Cabaret, as opposed to working for Scott Hansen, Nelson was able to see the full spectrum of comedy that Minneapolis had to offer. "It was a different type of crowd at Dudley's," she says. "It was more of a theater crowd, where the audiences were very smart and very supportive of the comics. They were much more patient. I could talk slower and tell a longer story. In the clubs, I learned how to get to the punch line quicker. I had to be more of a joke teller and less of a storyteller."

Nelson eventually moved away from stand-up comedy. She performed her own one-woman show, "Every Thought I've Ever Had," in the mid-nineties at the Hennepin Center for the Arts, before stepping out of the spotlight entirely, save for the occasional charity performance or one-off set. "The opportunities for comedy dried up," she says of her decision to get out of the business. "Once stand-up was on television, it was harder to get people to leave their houses and come watch us."

Ultimately, Nelson says she's proud of being able to open the door for other women to do stand-up, and she cherishes her own comedy memories.

"Between Susan Vass and myself and a handful of others, we could see that we were inspiring other women to perform," she says. "And that allowed all of us to get better. The newer female comics would look to us for advice, and we'd push ourselves to keep up with them. It was a unique time in my life, and I still treasure it today."

Kristin Andersen

Whereas some comedians envision performing for sold-out crowds and spend years clawing to get even the smallest amount of stage time in pursuit of their dreams, Kristin Andersen's motivation to get started in stand-up was slightly less noble, perhaps.

"I was watching a woman my age doing stand-up one night at the ETC," she recalls. "And thought, 'She just made fifty dollars to do that? I can make fifty dollars doing that.'"

Then a student at the University of Minnesota, Andersen got her start performing at Dudley Riggs's open mic nights, in between shifts at the club as a barista. While she may not have considered a career in comedy prior to that, Andersen quickly realized she had found her calling. "I knocked it out of the park," she says of her early experiences onstage. "It really felt like home. I was never going to be the ice-skating girl in high school. I was totally lost, dysfunctional, had no tools. So when I found comedy, I found a thing that made sense for me."

Karen Pickering remembers Andersen almost taking the stage by force. "In May 1985, there was a new person working at the box office at Dudley Riggs," she recalls. "Dudley listened to her talk with her razor-sharp tongue, just glaring into the eyeballs of patrons, and told her that she was going to be a part of his show. She had never done stand-up, but she never stopped after that."

Andersen was soon added to the cast of "What's So Funny About Being Female?" She looked up to her fellow performers at the time, but says she didn't feel they had the same dedication to the craft. "They were funny, but they weren't really trying to do anything bigger."

Feeling that the only way to grow as a comedian was to leave

Kristin Andersen was the headliner at Scott Hansen's Rib Tickler, a "Women's Comedy Night Club" in downtown Minneapolis, in May 1990.

the ETC, Andersen had a heart-to-heart with Dudley Riggs. She told him she was going to pursue stage time at the Comedy Gallery. "The shows at Dudley's club were really special. People were lined up around the block for this show, and it sold out every single time we did it. When I finally told Dudley that I was going to Scott Hansen's clubs, he told me, 'You know you don't have to do this.' But honestly I felt like there really wasn't another option."

By this time, the mid-eighties, Hansen had Comedy Gallery locations all over the Twin Cities. One night, Andersen went to the club on LaSalle Avenue, and she says Hansen was quick to bring her on board as a regular performer. "I was a pretty cute, young girl, so he was all over that," Andersen says. "But he gave me a ton of work, so I was very grateful for that."

Though she appreciated Hansen's connections and his ability to provide stage time, her opinion of the man himself is less than glowing. "If I were going to choose the most dysfunctional person in Minneapolis comedy, it would be Scott Hansen."

Andersen's stories about the treatment she received during her time working primarily for Hansen range from disrespectful to just plain weird. "There was another comedian named Colleen Kruse, and he pitted her against me," Andersen says. "I had no idea he did it until later, but it was just really juvenile and messed up."

She adds that he did other things to undermine her act. "He'd always want me to open for him, but then he'd have his brother Tom tell me that I couldn't do certain jokes. He couldn't do it himself, but he'd have Tom tell me that because he didn't want anyone to be too funny and have to follow it."

Andersen also had run-ins with other members of the original five. "One time I saw Louie Anderson at the Comedy Gallery and he told me, 'You could play my wife on TV,'" she remembers. "But then he told me I should stop doing the female jokes in my act. He told me I should stop for a few years, and if I felt like going back I could do it. At the time, I listened and thought a lot about whether I should be doing something different. Now, as a grown woman I think, 'We can talk about whatever we want to.' That was a pretty significant and common piece of feedback back then. If you're a female comedian, you shouldn't be talking about being a female."

On the road, things weren't much better. Andersen recalls enduring plenty of sexism and harassment at the hands of other comics as well as bookers. "I remember one time I was on the road and I was trying to get booked at some club down in the South. This guy gets on the phone with his southern accent and says, 'Kristin, I'm looking at you on this videotape, and hearing what's coming out of your mouth. And what I want to know is: is your hair still like that?'"

There was one member of the original five who Andersen says was always supportive of her career: Bill Bauer. "Bill took me out with him to some gigs; he was great," she recalls. "He would take people under his wing. He did that for me. I remember he taught me how to do callbacks [comedy lingo for referencing a joke from earlier in your set], and I got really good at it. He was so funny, because he told me that I was never allowed to show anyone else how to do it."

Even with her dicey relationships with most of the original five, Andersen does credit Hansen with allowing her to build a career at his clubs. She even recalls his support when she made the decision to move to Los Angeles. "I did my first open mic, and six months later I was doing comedy as my whole career," she remembers fondly. "And I got a lot of that work from him [Hansen]. The first time I went out to LA, he even wrote me a check for $500 and told me, 'Go get yourself on *The Tonight Show*.' That was very generous of him."

And if the personalities onstage and behind the scenes weren't consistently her favorite, Andersen always had positive things to say about the crowds. "Those Comedy Gallery crowds were just incredible. So supportive, and just so much fun."

Decades later, her friend and fellow comic Pickering says that Andersen is the same kind of comic she always was.

"Her style hasn't changed. She just talks about life the way it happens, and you don't want to get in her way."

Stephanie Hodge

In addition to being one of the driving forces behind the Comedy Cabaret, Stephanie Hodge was a pretty incredible performer in her own right.

An actor by trade, Hodge had never considered taking the stage to try stand-up, even when she worked at Dudley Riggs during the inception of the Minneapolis Comedy All-Stars. But it's amazing how a mere fifty dollars can change the course of someone's entire career.

Stephanie Hodge. (Courtesy of Stephanie Hodge)

☆ STEPHANIE HODGE ☆

"My friend Doreen King one night bet me fifty dollars that I wouldn't get up and try stand-up," Hodge recalls. "It wasn't something I was really interested in, but hey, it's fifty dollars."

Instead of working on joke structure or drilling into her own experiences for material, Hodge decided to stick with what she knew best: acting. "I wrote a monologue as though I was an actress playing the part of a stand-up comedian," she says. "And when I got up and performed, I did really, really well. Then the next fifty times I got up and did it, I sucked."

Despite the lack of early success, Hodge kept at it, all while working through the challenges of being female in a male-driven industry. "There was so much sexism and misogyny at the time," she recalls. "When I finally started to get better and get booked on the road, I was like the freak show act. Like, 'Step right up and see the woman!' People would be like, 'What? A female? They aren't funny!'"

While many women in the field got angry and pushed back against this type of small-minded thinking, Hodge decided to use the stigma to her advantage. "I wore body-con dresses, stuff from the 1940s and 1950s, and big, spiky heels," Hodge says. "I had platinum blonde hair, and pretty much looked like a pinup girl on wheels. My attitude was that if people were going to make fun of me or not take me seriously because I'm a woman, then I'd give them a cartoon character that they could accept. So I did that, and just did whatever I could to get more stage time."

Kristin Andersen says that Hodge's character helped her stand out from the pack, but her talent was undeniable. "Stephanie was a funny broad," she says. "Back then, she was like Mary Tyler Moore with a smoke and a martini."

Karen Pickering, who had been spending quite a bit of time at the Comedy Cabaret, became fast friends with Hodge. "She was always an incredible talent, and still is," Pickering recalls. "She had a Marilyn Monroe look, with the bleached blonde hair and pouty lips, and heels that would poke your eye out in the front row. Everything she did just slayed."

Her approach paid off. Hodge was able to make herself stand out in the increasingly crowded community of comedians on the local scene. However, her success onstage didn't protect her from harsh judgments from other women, thanks to her role as one of the owners of the Comedy Cabaret. "I went to Scott and Scott [Hansen and Novotny] and really tried to push the idea of bringing in more women performers," she says. "Not just women, but performers whom women could identify with. But with those two, if a comedian wasn't a certain type of performer, they weren't given stage time."

One of these performers, ironically, was Pickering. "Scott Novotny wouldn't book me. He didn't think I was funny," she remembers. "So I took his comedy class, and Scott Hansen ended up booking me. It was a riot."

With the lack of support from many of the men on the scene, including her Comedy Cabaret partners, Hodge says many women didn't feel they could speak out against that for fear of retribution. Instead, they turned their anger toward her. "There are some women who were in comedy during that time who had grudges against me. Some of them probably still do," Hodge says. "I tried to tell them I wasn't trying to hold anyone back. I wanted more women to perform. I wasn't afraid of them taking something away from me. I wasn't threatened by them. They weren't like me."

Despite those differences, Hodge did have a tremendous relationship with her fellow female comedians in town, and she believes that collectively they changed the perception of women, both locally and nationally. "Comedy wasn't open or friendly as a whole," she says. "Women from our town dispelled that theory. We were supportive of each other. If a woman wasn't being given equal stage time, we'd get upset. Some of them chose to be quiet about it when they saw that happening. That wasn't me. Early on, I let people push me around, and then I didn't. I started telling people who I am and what I wanted to achieve. I made a bad impression on some of those people because of it."

Karen Pickering

By now it's pretty clear that sexism and misogyny were common themes for female comedians in Minneapolis during the eighties. Whether that meant lack of opportunity, unfair competition, or limitations on what they could talk about onstage, the women of this era almost unanimously say that sexism hindered them in some way. That is, almost all of them.

"When I think back on that decade, I think about how lucky I was as a woman in comedy because there were so many opportunities," says Karen Pickering. "But I know other people thought we were treated like shit."

Pickering got her start in 1984 performing at the Comedy Cabaret. Unlike other performers, who usually stayed closely connected to one club, however, Pickering didn't allow herself to be tied down anywhere. "The Comedy Cabaret started booking me sometimes after I'd done their open mic. Then I started doing Scott Hansen's open

Karen Pickering. (Photo by Ann Marsden)

mic over at the Comedy Gallery. I also worked in the basement of Boomers [previously Mickey Finn's] with Bill Bauer. I was doing all of that at once, so I was getting a lot of work."

While there was plenty of stage time to be had, Pickering was still making ends meet by working in corporate America. That, she says, is where she saw the real sexism. "The comedy world wasn't nearly as gross to me as what I was seeing at my day job," she recalls. "Guys thinking they could just say and do whatever they wanted with secretaries and things like that. It was bad."

Comedy was Pickering's creative outlet, an escape from her normal daily life. Being onstage meant the opportunity to talk about what mattered to her, and what she found funny. "The stuff I was talking about was the standard dating, breaking up stuff that was going on in my life," she remembers. "But I was also obsessed with the First Ladies. I wasn't political. I didn't want to talk politics. But I loved talking about how worried I was about Nancy Reagan, and how if she wasn't careful one of those Air Force One choppers was going to suck her in and break her skinny little neck. If she died, who was going to make the decisions in this country?"

Kristin Andersen recalls one specific joke that she felt really captured Pickering as a performer. "Karen did a joke about the size of foot-long hot dogs at the state fair," Andersen recalls. "She'd say something like, 'Must have been measured by a man. It was only ten inches long.' Years later I saw her at a gig and begged her to do that joke."

One of the things that set Pickering apart from other comedians—male or female—was that she was a joke-writing machine. "I'd carry a little briefcase with a recorder in it and record all of my sets," she says. "And then I'd go back and write new material. I was just getting crazy with it. But when I worked on new jokes, I was more about working with the guys than women. I would think, 'We're going to sit around and make jokes about our periods? This is bullshit.'"

"She was the hardest-working comedian in town," says Andersen. "I don't know anyone who wrote so much or wanted to give more to the community."

Although she was bouncing between clubs, Pickering got to a point where she felt it was in her best interest to branch out from her "home" club of the Comedy Cabaret. "I was very devoted to the Comedy Cabaret because I was good friends with Stephanie Hodge. And I was driving Scott [Novotny] crazy because I was being really possessive of his wife. So that was one reason I figured I should find a new place. Plus the crowd [of comedians] that was performing there was drinking way too much. I knew I needed to stop the binging, and being in that group wasn't going to help me if I ever wanted to get sober."

At that point, Scott Hansen invited her to become more of a regular in his clubs, and Pickering jumped at the opportunity. She stayed fairly tight with the Comedy Gallery crowd for a while, until she heard about the "What's So Funny About Being Female?" show at Dudley Riggs's ETC. "I'd hang out with the Hansen crowd most of the time, and then go over to Dudley's for the open mic," Pickering says. "When I heard they were going to start doing an all-women show, and they asked me to be a part of it, it was really cool because it meant a steady check and the ability to stay in one place for a while."

Still, it took Pickering some time to mesh with the other comedians in the "What's So Funny About Being Female?" shows. "I had never worked with mom-type women before," she recalls. "I was like twenty-seven or twenty-eight, and all these women I was working with were like in their forties. And they were control freaks. I felt like they were mom-ing me all the time."

Eventually she found common ground with the other women, and she performed as part of the collective for several runs of the show. "I loved that group. We were together five nights a week for three months. Honestly, to this day I can't believe we lived through it," she says.

In 1987, Pickering took a comedy class at the HaHa Club, which had replaced the Comedy Cabaret. The class was taught by Joel Hodgson, whose stature as a comedian towered over the rest of the Minnesota comedy scene. After performing for Hodgson and working with other talented comics like Colleen Kruse, Josh Weinstein, and Ken Bradley, Pickering decided to make the move to New York.

"There weren't many women in Minnesota doing comedy," she says plainly. "If you wanted to make it back then, you had to move out to Los Angeles or New York. So I moved out and gave it a try."

One night after a show in New York, a friend of Pickering's offered to have her boyfriend walk Pickering to her car. Pickering agreed, but then she was attacked and raped by the man. The trauma of the incident brought her back to Minnesota, where she put stand-up on the back burner for many years. She went to therapy to work through the stress of the incident and quit the nightclub circuit altogether. While she still performed at a few small corporate gigs in private settings for a brief period, she eventually stepped out of the comedy scene entirely, until years later when her teenage kids discovered their mom's comedy past and encouraged her to get back onstage.

"There were so many fascinating women I had met before I moved," she says. "Back then, the guys weren't afraid to be edgy onstage, but most of the women felt like they needed to be polite. The women I connected with, like Lizz Winstead, were so incredible and funny and weren't afraid to be just as edgy. When I got back and saw that there were more women who had that same attitude, it made me want to get back to performing. It felt like the path we had laid down years earlier was being followed by a new group of women, and they inspired me in the same way a generation of female comedians had inspired me years prior."

Once she got back onstage, she began to remember why she fell in love with performing in the first place, and ultimately she returned to the open mic and club circuit. Today, Pickering produces her own shows, offering female performers an opportunity to find their voices onstage—much as she had been offered the same opportunity years before.

Colleen Kruse

When Colleen Kruse was nineteen, she became pregnant with her daughter. At that point, life became about figuring out how to pay the bills and take care of her kid. It wasn't easy.

"I was in the welfare system," Kruse recalls. "I had a social worker who was tasked with helping me figure my way out of the welfare system. He asked me, 'What did you want to do before you became a welfare mother?' And I told him that I wanted to be a stand-up comic."

While the dream had been there from a young age, Kruse didn't actually get onstage for the first time until she was twenty-one. "Joel Hodgson came back to town after he did his *SNL* performances and facilitated a writing class," she says. "It was me, Ken Bradley, Josh Weinstein, Roman Dicaire. There were a lot of really great comedians in that group, but I was still too afraid to perform."

Kruse eventually found her grit, and in 1989 she got onstage for the first time, at the HaHa Club. She was an instant success. At first. "I didn't tank until my fourth time onstage," Kruse notes with a laugh.

She soon became a regular at the HaHa Club, but she was still only really a casual performer. "I was focused on raising my daughter, plus I had a full-time job," Kruse says. "It was just something to do for fun. The idea of making money [doing comedy] never really crossed my mind. It just felt like a huge leap."

Then Scott Hansen called Kruse one night when she was in the back room of the HaHa Club. She was shocked that he even knew who she was, let alone wanted her to perform at his club. "It was really surreal to me," she says. "He asked me to come over and do a set at his Riverplace club."

Other comics have talked about paying their dues in order to get stage time with Hansen; Kruse laughs at the notion. "There is no such thing as paying your dues," she says. "Either you're funny or you're not. If he was having people set up chairs or whatever else, he was probably just looking for someone to set up the chairs for free."

By the time Kruse started performing regularly, the landscape of funny women in the Twin Cities was fairly well formed. "There were a lot of great women in town," Kruse remembers. "Priscilla Nelson, Maxine Jeffries, Kristin Andersen, Dora Harris, Phyllis Wright. There were probably fifteen female headliners in town when I started working for Scott. And they were true, fully developed headliners. I had been watching them since I was a teenager."

With her buzz-cut hairstyle and bold, unfiltered material, Kruse stood out from her peers almost immediately. "I'd walk up onstage and say, 'My name is Colleen, and I'm a liberal Christian feminist. In some crowds I can say I'm a liberal, and in others I can say I'm a Christian, and neither of those things will be polarizing. But if I say I'm a feminist, I get lumped into this hairy-armpitted, lesbian, separatist, man-hating category. And that's not fair because you don't have to be a lesbian to hate men.' That was my opener. At that point I could say whatever I wanted."

Recognizing the success of the "What's So Funny About Being Female?" shows at Dudley Riggs's ETC, Scott Hansen began cultivating a new group of female performers that included Kruse, along with people like Jackie Kashian and Maria Bamford. It didn't take long before Kruse had a consistent spot in Hansen's rotation. "I opened for everyone," she says. "Paula Poundstone, Judy Tenuta, Diane Ford, Emo Philips, Andrew Dice Clay, Pauly Shore, Henny Youngman. I opened for everyone because Scott had everyone coming through his clubs."

Despite her success locally, things didn't always go so well when Kruse went on the road. "There was a lot of sexism," she says. "It was

Colleen Kruse with Henny Youngman at Scott Hansen's Comedy Gallery at Galtier Plaza. (Courtesy of Colleen Kruse)

easier to get booked but harder to do the work. Once you get the booking doesn't mean it's going to go smoothly. I remember once I did a show at Westward Ho [in Grand Forks, North Dakota] and the owner of the club followed me back to my room with a German shepherd. He had a key and just let himself in. He asked if I wanted to come walk his dog with him, and I said no thank you. Then he started talking about how I had such a great show, and he doesn't really think women are funny and all of this. So I picked up the Bible and started reading to him. I just acted like a religious zealot. I figured the weirder I could get, the better. I sat there and read for a good fifteen minutes before he finally left."

Though she walked away from that incident physically unscathed, another night she wasn't so fortunate. "I was assaulted once. That was an awful, horrible chapter for me. If you're a female comic, you stick out like a sore thumb. You're a mouthy woman. I was targeted that night because I was a comedian and I was onstage. I was visible. I really didn't go on the road after that."

Kruse enjoyed performing, but she never had any serious thoughts about "making it" in comedy beyond Minnesota. That is, until she opened for Roseanne. "One day Scott called me and invited me to do a guest set in front of Roseanne," she remembers. "I didn't know it, but Jimmy Miller, Dennis Miller's brother, was in the audience. After the show, we started talking, and he told me I should come out to LA. I told him that was never going to happen, because I had to get up the next day at 5 AM, get ready for work, get my kids ready, take the bus, and be at work by 6:15 AM. Then I was going to work until 4, feed my kids dinner, be out the door at 7, be back home at 11, and then do it all over again the next day."

Undeterred, Miller worked his connections and called Kruse a few weeks later. "He called and told me he had an audition for me," she says. "So I flew out and auditioned to be the replacement white girl on *In Living Color*. At that point Jimmy became my manager. I got three development deals for sitcoms in the nineties. None of them went anywhere, but it changed my life. I bought a house and a car, and I paid off some debt."

Kruse transitioned out of stand-up by the early 2000s, plying her talents instead as a columnist for *The Rake* (a monthly magazine based in Minneapolis) and as a local talk radio host. Though she found her way to other opportunities that allowed her to showcase her story-telling abilities, she always credits stand-up comedy as the reason she got to where she did.

"It changed my life," she says proudly of stand-up comedy. "So much of my life is directly related to me being a stand-up comic, and the opportunities I got back then."

··· 16 ···

The Bubble Bursts

Entering the 1990s, comedy was as hot as ever. Some of the most popular comics who had made frequent visits to the Twin Cities, including Roseanne Barr and Jerry Seinfeld, signed sitcom deals, following in the footsteps of Bob Newhart, Robin Williams, Bill Cosby, and others. Comedy specials were the hottest properties on HBO and Showtime. And locally, thousands of comedy fans were filling seats all over the Twin Cities practically every night of the week. In fact, comedy might have been getting a little *too* hot.

Matt Fugate was a comic who began appearing on local stages around 1987. He performed in a few of Hansen's rooms, but his refusal to "pay his dues" in the Hansen system led him to find work outside of the Comedy Gallery empire. Fortunately, there was no shortage of opportunities. "After Scott moved his club out of J. R.'s, they kept the comedy room open and it was just run by other comedians," Fugate recalls. "So you had that, you had Dave Wood's Rib Tickler, the HaHa Club; there were plenty of places to perform. And then you had other places that decided to bring in comics."

Those "other places" included an assortment of makeshift stages at venues ranging from restaurants to airlines. For Fugate, one of his strangest experiences around this time came with the opening of local casinos. "There were companies that would charter these buses up to the casinos and back, and they would hire comedians to entertain on the way up, and then have a joke telling contest on the way back," Fugate recalls. "Median age on this bus has got to be maybe sixty-five. Plus there is nothing like trying to entertain, statistically, a bunch of losers on the way back. But they'd serve beer, and I'd get up and try to do a few minutes and make some money. So when people tell you they tried comedy everywhere, they meant it."

Whether it was buses, casinos, or clubs, it's not an exaggeration to say that comedy was everywhere. But that was all about to change.

At that point, Hansen's empire—and to be clear, it was an empire—included the Comedy Gallery at Riverplace, which was selling out all 300 seats upward of six nights a week, and the Comedy Gallery at Galtier Plaza in St. Paul, which was packing in close to 400 people per show anywhere between five and seven nights per week. Add in another 250 seats at Mandarin Yen, which Hansen was booking full time; a Comedy Gallery Uptown location at Williams Bar; his all-female comedy club, Scott Hansen's Rib Tickler; the occasional show at places like the Guthrie Theater; and a handful of one-nighters, and comedians were looking at around 6,000 seats to fill each week. "These were people who paid to be at these shows," notes Hansen.

So how did the bubble burst? According to Hansen, it didn't. "The bubble was popped," he says plainly. "A club called the Funny Bone [not to be confused with a club of the same name that had occupied Williams Bar before Hansen took over] came into town and put an ad in the paper that said, 'Call for your free tickets! National comedy headline acts!' The acts they had might have been from around the country, but they weren't headliners."

Hansen had developed a model that sold comedy as the main attraction. His clubs were custom-built for people who wanted to see a comedy show, with proper sight lines, excellent sound, and a theater-like experience that no one else in town could match. "Mall of America opened a club next [Knuckleheads] that did the same thing. They were offering free comedy. They didn't care, because they were selling booze, while I was trying to sell tickets. That just killed off a lot of our business. It didn't matter that we were putting on better shows with better talent. People saw that they could get into someplace for free and didn't see the point of paying us."

With this surge of new clubs coming into his territory, Hansen's former partner Louis Lee was about to become another direct rival.

"There was a club called Dave Wood's Rib Tickler in Minneapolis," Lee recalls. "They were going bankrupt, and they came to me and offered to sell me half of the club. I said, 'I just did this with Scott. If I buy half of the club, that makes you whole, but you still have no clue how to make money. I'm not going to help make you whole when you don't know how to make this thing work.'"

So Lee waited, knowing the club was likely to go out of business sooner or later. Once it did, he made his move. "I went to the landlord and struck a deal to open a restaurant and comedy club," he says. "The owner didn't think comedy was going to work in that space. So I convinced him I was going to try something new. I also told him that even though Scott owned everything in comedy locally at that point, he had made a lot of enemies and things would crumble for him."

As it turned out, Hansen also put in a bid on the space, but the owner chose to make a deal with Lee. That day, Acme Comedy Company was born.

Still reeling from his experience with Hansen, Lee insisted that he didn't want to be involved in the comedy portion of the business. "The only reason why I wanted it is because they already had a restaurant, a bar, and a club," he says. "I brought in a comedian [Kristin Andersen], and made her the same type of deal we did with Scott. She would book the room and keep the door, and I would run the bar and the restaurant."

Although he wasn't interested in booking the comedy himself, Lee saw that the scene was reaching a turning point. "By that time, I could see there were too many clubs in town and not enough good comics," Lee recalls. "It was a bunch of middle-aged men and women who wanted to quit their jobs and try to become comics. Plus, Scott Hansen had told all of his comics that if they worked for him they couldn't come and work for me. He had something like fifty rooms at the time, so they didn't want to lose all that work. We had to think differently."

Whereas Lee's previous deal with Hansen had worked due to Hansen's cash flow and existing relationships with comedians, Kristin Andersen didn't have the same pull when it came to booking talent. "She came to me and said, 'I don't have any money to hire comics.' She said she wanted to headline the club maybe three or four times over the next few months to cut costs, and I said no. I knew that wasn't going to work and we had to offer something different. She insisted that she couldn't afford it, so I said you got to go."

In her place, Lee hired Becky Johnson, who had been booking comedy at Williams Bar before Hansen took over. "I told Becky we needed to start from scratch," Lee recalls. "We needed a new audience, because the way the other clubs were trying to bring in people wasn't going to last."

Lee had found success in his other ventures, so he clearly had vision that others didn't. He decided to lower the age limit at his new club to eighteen, and he took away the requirement that customers purchase drinks. "I wanted to get the college kids in," he says. "I knew they didn't drink, but they had only seen shitty comedy at that point. I knew if I could get them in and expose them to a new group of talent, in four years I'd have my first group of twenty-two-year-olds with disposable income who would come back and spend money."

That logic was compelling but risky. Even if he could build a new audience by going after a different age group, it didn't answer the question of how to attract new talent. Once again, he decided to start from scratch. "I started doing a free weekly open mic night, and then we started doing an amateur contest during the summer," Lee recalls. "The idea was to build a new group of comedians while I was building the audience simultaneously. And if everything went right, in four years I'd have my first batch of really good emcees that people would pay to come see."

Knowing the plan was going to take time to develop, Lee decided to pursue the same approach as other clubs when it came to luring audiences and combating Hansen's empire. "I'd throw out thousands of free tickets every week, so that nobody had to pay for it," Lee says. "When you make your money based on ticket sales, and the people aren't there, you don't have anything. I figured if I could get people in the doors, I could sell them food and drinks to survive while we developed that audience."

Josh Weinstein, who had been a Hansen regular for quite some time, offered a different take on the state of the scene at that point in the early nineties. "I don't know that the talent wasn't good enough in town; it's just that everyone had seen it all," Weinstein says. "There were maybe twenty comics who made up most of the feature sets. If you went to the clubs a few times a year, chances were pretty good that you'd end up seeing everyone's acts."

Alex Cole, however, believes it was absolutely the lack of talent that caused the bubble to burst. "I could see acts in the early nineties who were just sort of taking up space onstage," he recalls, "acts who really didn't work hard and who shouldn't be there. I remember one time I worked with someone on the road who was a middle act and had maybe twenty minutes of material. Two years later, I'm seeing him headline one of these clubs in town, and he's doing the exact same twenty minutes verbatim. That's when I knew times were a-changing. The new comics coming in hadn't had the experience of getting on the road and building a set and working hard, and you could see it."

The comedy club culture as a whole had begun to shift. Audiences still showed up, but now they were less interested in comedy and more interested in a cheap night out. "I could feel it in the crowds," says Weinstein. "You could tell they were there because their office got a bunch of free tickets, not because the comedy club was a cool place to go."

Soon after, the casinos began throwing massive amounts of money at major names, essentially eliminating club owners like Hansen from contention for those big-time acts. "I couldn't compete with their prices," Hansen says. "The casinos could pay Seinfeld in a night what I could pay him for a week, or even double. At that point I had eight people working in our offices calling to solicit free tickets just to try to keep up."

Alex Jackson, who had several stints in California before heading back to Minneapolis, says television was the culprit behind the comedy club burst. "At first you'd only have stand-up shows on TV, like *Evening at the Improv*, once a week, so coming to the clubs was still the main way people saw comedy," Jackson says. "But then once you had the advent of cable, people were being fed comedy 24/7. They started coming to the comedy clubs and acting like they were at home watching it on TV. During my shows I would actually explain it to them. I'd say, 'Hey, I can see you. This is not a TV. If you're watching me at home on TV, you can tell me I suck. If you do it here? I'm gonna talk about you.' People would eat that up when I'd do it as a joke, but it really was different, and you could feel it."

Tom Hansen agrees that cable played a role in the downslide, but he also questioned the quality of the comedians getting onstage. "People were getting onstage who shouldn't have been," Tom says bluntly. "Let's put it this way: there were acts that were doing fifteen minutes at our club, and thirty to forty-five minutes at other clubs. People weren't seeing as good of a product. After a while, it kind of felt like going to watch karaoke, unfortunately."

The seats were still getting filled, but the money didn't follow. Between the cutting back of talent and the financial strain, Hansen began closing some of his comedy rooms. "I scaled way back," he recalls. "It got to a point where I didn't want to deal with the business side of things anymore."

Stephanie Hodge, who had left town just as things were beginning to saturate, sees the bubble burst as a combination of factors. "More clubs, more comedy—it was everywhere," she says. "And the more diluted things seem to get, the less special they start to feel. I don't know if that was everyone's sense, but to me it felt less exciting, less new, less interesting."

Hodge doesn't believe the talent pool had dried up, however. Rather, she says the old guard didn't provide the same opportunities to newer comics that they had years before. "The talent pool remained fresh and large. New people were coming in all the time. Someone would leave, and someone else would be there to step up and take their place," Hodge says. "The thing about it is that in comedy, everyone needs to start. And everyone in Minneapolis lost patience with those who needed to start. We did not afford those people the same patience we afforded ourselves, and that's because the business had gotten so big. It wasn't anybody trying to hold anybody else back or anything. It just became such a big business."

In October 1991, Hansen announced that he was closing the Comedy Gallery at Riverplace. Although he continued to operate the St.

Paul location and promoted shows in the smaller rooms, this closure was the clear sign that change was in the air. For Hansen, however, the change was a relief. "I realized I could still perform and book shows, but I didn't need to worry about the financial piece of it. It was taking a toll on my health, and I wasn't able to spend as much time with my family. It just wasn't worth it."

In 1992, there were seven stand-alone comedy clubs in the Twin Cities, and dozens of additional stages hosted within restaurants and bars across town. By 1994, only two of the comedy clubs remained—and neither was owned by Hansen. The boom was over.

As the available stage time began to dry up, so did the money for comedians. "It used to be that I could put three comedians on the road for a week," Tom Hansen says. "The headliner would make $1,500, the feature would get $800 to $1,000, and the opener would be making about $300 to $325. By the time clubs were closing, headliners were working for half of that, so it was hard to make any money. And the money never really recovered after that."

While stand-up comedy as a whole managed to limp along, Hodge described the situation best: "It lost its glitter."

Hansen's decision to step back from his role as a promoter would open the door for new individuals to step up and attempt to cash in on what was left of the once-mighty comedy craze. While some, like Lee, were still committed to the art of comedy, others were merely looking for a quick cash grab and promoting shows with less-than-stellar acts. Fortunately, the early stand-up pioneers who had made the Twin Cities a comedy hub would not go silently into the night.

··· 17 ···

Aftermath and Legacy

By the mid-1990s, Twin Cities comedy wasn't a pretty sight, to say the least. But there was still a small but dedicated local following.

According to Fancy Ray McCloney, the crowds had dwindled, but those who were coming out to the clubs were the true comedy fans. "There were definitely fewer people coming, but the ones who were coming to the clubs were there because they really loved comedy," McCloney says. "Before that, people would come to the comedy club because it was the place to hang out. Now people who took the time to come were doing it because they actually wanted to see live comedy."

While McCloney and others were still working the last of the rooms Scott Hansen continued to book, Hansen's stand-alone clubs had shuttered, leaving very sparse opportunities for stage time. Meanwhile, Louis Lee was struggling to make it as the new guy on the block. "Those first three years of Acme I lost about $150,000," he recalls. "I had to call my family and keep asking them for more money, and amazingly they agreed to give it to me. I had a small kitchen staff, and I basically did everything except tell jokes."

As he worked to rebuild the comedy scene, Lee decided that the days of choosing sides for comics needed to come to an end. "Mall of America opened Knuckleheads Comedy Club, and it was just us and them," Lee says. "So I went down there in 1993 and met with the booker, Rich Miller [his brother Dennis had been a regular of the Comedy Gallery empire before making it big on *Saturday Night Live*].

We decided we needed to do what's good for comedy. We needed to share acts. Let's not play games; let's give them the stage time they need to get better. I said we would close Acme on Sundays for their open mic night, and in return they would close Mondays for us. We had to work together. Once we did, Minneapolis became a fast-growing talent town, even with only two clubs."

Lee's strategy and investment eventually started to pay off. The crowds he had spent years cultivating began coming to the club for dinner and drinks. The open mic performers and contest participants had provided Acme with a solid base of emcees and feature acts. And Lee's determination had turned Acme from the outlier of the Twin Cities comedy scene into the main attraction.

As for the original five, they all continued to find varying degrees of success into the nineties. Louie Anderson, of course, appeared in movies like *Coming to America,* created the animated television show *Life with Louie,* and wrote multiple best-selling books, in addition to maintaining an impressive touring schedule. Jeff Gerbino, who had moved back to Minnesota in 1990 to raise his family, was hosting local radio shows and still finding time to perform around town at corporate events and the occasional one-nighter. Bill Bauer also returned to Minnesota from Los Angeles in 1990 for family, after having found success working on TV scripts and continuing to tour around the country. Alex Cole had moved away from stand-up and instead focused his energy on the theater, fulfilling the observations of his fellow comedians who had always referred to him as an "actor" onstage.

Cole did get into the business side of comedy for a short period, however, partnering with Hansen to book comedians at colleges. "After I got pushed out of colleges, I decided that maybe I should start booking comedy," Cole recalls. "The idea being that my connections could help get Scott's comedians into the colleges."

Unfortunately, while the two had plenty of history together and a mutual respect as performers, the same couldn't be said of their business partnership. "It worked out as far as making money was concerned," Cole continues, "but the way things were handled didn't work between us. I don't really want to go into it too much, but let's just say we had a problem over money, and I quit."

Aside from being a promoter, albeit with a smaller footprint than he once had, Hansen encountered some significant health problems that kept him out of the limelight for several years. Still, he would surface from time to time for the occasional show.

By this point, any one of the five could have walked away from comedy completely, having cemented their spots on the Mount Rushmore of Twin Cities stand-up. But the itch to perform brought them together once again.

As Scott Novotny tells it, "After I came back from Los Angeles—this would have been in the early nineties—a bunch of us got together and saw that there was a comedy club out in Maplewood. We hated what the guy running this club was doing. He was taking openers and headlining them. The audiences would see these really crappy shows and never come back again. So a bunch of us got together and proposed to the owners that they should oust the guy running it and let us do our thing instead."

That "thing" would be the Minnesota Comedy Club. Located in one of Hansen's former Comedy Gallery rooms, the club became something of a comedy co-op made up of those same names that had been responsible for building the local scene years prior.

Scott Hansen, Tom Hansen, Tom's wife Holly Hensen, Jeff Gerbino, Bill Bauer, Scott Novotny, Rox Tarrant, Dean Johnson, Maxine Jeffries, and Ric McCloud joined forces and created a club that was equal parts nostalgic throwback and a platform for new comics looking for stage time. The group was aiming to recapture a simpler time in comedy, when each act only worried about getting onstage and having fun.

"It was a lot of fun," Novotny reflects. "We put on some really great shows. If you were the headliner for the weekend, you could kind of design your own show. Most of all it was just fun to have all of us back together. We even ended up playing together in a softball league, which Scott set up."

"Honestly, one of the biggest reasons I think we did it was to try to make Bill happy again," says Tom Hansen. "He had just gotten kicked out of LA and moved back to town, and he was having some trouble with his son and school. It was a way to help get him back

Rox Tarrant (far right) and Scott Novotny (second from left) at the Minnesota Comedy Club. (Courtesy of Rox Tarrant)

onstage, and it worked out really well. It gave all these comics a place they could work without worrying about all the politics and stuff and get some chops. It was also great because there were a lot of really good comics who weren't getting stage time at Acme. Guys like Mark Poolos, Mike Brody, and Michael Thorne all came through the club, and they're all doing really well still today."

Looking to create the only club in town that was run by comedians, for comedians, the group decided to operate cooperatively. Rox Tarrant was elected group president. Tarrant had started performing in 1995 and was a finalist in Acme's "Funniest Person Contest" that year. She was very familiar with the local comedy scene, having been a frequent visitor of Scott Hansen's Comedy Galleries in previous years.

"I would follow Wild Bill Bauer. I went to all of his shows and thought he was just hilarious," Tarrant recalls. "After I did well in the Acme contest, Bill became sort of my comedy mentor. He helped me the most of anyone in comedy, and I learned a lot from him. He introduced me to Scott Hansen, who started booking me for shows and giving me opportunities. So when the time came for this group of bigwigs to start this club, I was very fortunate that Bill asked me to be a part of it."

The club was an artistic and commercial success, producing quality shows and attracting sellout crowds. But, according to Tarrant, old habits started to rear their ugly heads once again. "They were a bunch of dysfunctional babies," Tarrant says with a laugh about her co-op colleagues. "It was very stressful dealing with all these personalities."

Hansen, Bauer, and Gerbino, in particular, were bickering like they had back at Mickey Finn's. "They were always up to something," Tarrant recalls. "I never understood it. They were vicious. They would really try to undermine each other over every dumb little thing. The bookings, the way we promoted the club, the way we would put our best foot forward to present the club. It was anything and everything."

While Tarrant says some members of the group, like Novotny, were happy to have her in charge, others tried to undermine her role as group president. Even Bauer, who had been the one to take Tarrant under his wing and teach her the ropes of both performing and promoting shows, eventually snapped and fell back into old habits. "After about a year, Bill Bauer got on his high horse and screamed at me, 'By god, Rox, I'm going to get you ousted from this club! You'll never work another day!' It was just ridiculous," she says. "Bill threatened me many times. That was just kind of who Bill was. It was very different getting to know them as people as opposed to seeing them onstage."

Eventually, Tarrant decided she'd had enough of the toxicity of the promoter life and stepped down. "We had a meeting, and I finally told them all to grow up," she says. "I'm very glad I had this experience, but it was really hard on me."

With Tarrant out, the rest of the group decided they were more interested in performing than managing the business end of the club.

So they turned that piece over to Tom Hansen. "I kind of got stuck with it," he says with a laugh.

Conflicts and politics aside, Tarrant agrees that the club was a success. "I think we gave them [the other comedy clubs in town] a run for their money," she says proudly. "I think they were all waiting to see how we would do, and we were quite successful. We filled a niche and came about at the right time. We flourished because there was a need for an alternative to Acme, which was hiring mostly national headliners and using locals as emcees and features."

The irony that the originals were now being viewed as the alternative and the underdog in the comedy scene was not lost on Tarrant. But she says the structure and people behind the scenes were the difference makers. "It was run by comedians, for comedians. We knew how to do it."

As the 2000s came along, the original five all continued to write and perform individually. Then, in 2004, something happened that many had waited to see for more than twenty years: the original five came back together.

Hansen, Bauer, Gerbino, Anderson, and Cole agreed to do a weekend of shows at the Hotel Sofitel in Bloomington, a room where Hansen was still occasionally booking shows. To promote the event, the gang sat down with a reporter from the *Star Tribune* at Market Bar-B-Que, one of their go-to after-show hangouts, to reflect on where they each landed.

"Comics aren't easy to work with," Hansen said when asked about leaving the business side of comedy. "Now I don't have to worry about who's working at what location. I don't have to take any more calls about some comedian who was hitting on an employee or something else. I found that I could just work with what I do as a comic. I can do a lot less work and spend more time with my family."

Bauer was still hitting the road hard, performing upward of two hundred stand-up dates a year. "There's not been a time in the last twenty-five years that I've thought for one second that I wanted to do something else," he said.

Cole, on the other hand, was finding his way back to comedy after his run in the theater. "I can't do anything else; I have no skills," he

All five originals, together again—as featured on the poster that was included with the CD of the event

Scott Hansen onstage at the twenty-five-year anniversary show featuring the original five. (Courtesy of Scott Hansen)

Louie Anderson (left) and Alex Cole (right) at the twenty-five-year anniversary show. (Courtesy of Scott Hansen)

joked. "I love waking up every day and looking at my calendar and seeing I have a show date."

Gerbino had settled into his next phase of life, taking the time to appreciate all he had accomplished. "People ask me, 'How'd you do?' I don't know. When you compare me to Louie, not so good," he said. "But I'll go toe to toe with the other ninety percent of working comics. My house is paid for, my son goes to Minnehaha Academy, and my daughter goes to Columbia. I've got two hundred acres of land that's paid for. I'm doing all right."

Of course, Anderson had secured his A-list Hollywood status by this time. However, he had undergone a significant open-heart surgery less than a year earlier. That experience, he said, reminded him of where he came from, why he wanted to do comedy, and the importance of performing alongside the original five once again. "I came back here to rediscover what I had discovered twenty-five years

Clockwise from top left: Louie Anderson, Jeff Gerbino, Scott Hansen, Alex Cole, and Bill Bauer, one week prior to Bauer's death. (Courtesy of Scott Hansen)

ago, which is this young, great, loving, optimistic kid who loved to work and do stand-up. This reunion thing is part of the process of me fixing my life. I started out with these guys, and I guess all of us are still connected. We really did create comedy here; there's no doubt about that."

As for the shows themselves, unsurprisingly they were a massive success. "I had the time of my life at those shows," recalls Cole. "And we had a hell of a show. At that point Louie, he didn't have to do this, but he let us all split the money evenly. He didn't have to do that. With where he was in his career and all that, he could have taken a good chunk of change, but he didn't."

Anderson was less concerned about the money and more interested in rediscovering something that had maybe gotten lost along the way.

"It was very emotional for me," he recalls. "I always tell comics to enjoy the journey. Because once the journey is over and you get to the place you think you need to be, it'll never be the same. Those reunion shows reminded me of that. No matter how hard you try to reminisce, it's never the same. But it was a chance to celebrate and revel in those moments, and to remember where we all came from and how we all got there."

Epilogue

In the years that followed, Scott Hansen gradually moved away from his role as the A-list comedy promoter in the Twin Cities, and Louis Lee began to fill the niche. However, that didn't happen overnight.

The talent pool had become a puddle. According to Lee, all the talented comics had migrated west to pursue TV and acting opportunities, leaving a handful of middle-aged men who were interested in exploring stand-up as an outlet for their midlife crises.

Fortunately, Acme Comedy Club began attracting a younger, more creative group of comics in the early 2000s, with names like Mitch Hedberg, Nick Swardson, and Maria Bamford becoming mainstays. A second boom was born, and younger audiences began flocking to the club.

Major national names in comedy, like Jim Gaffigan, Patton Oswalt, Lewis Black, and Louis C.K., made Minneapolis a regular stop on their tours. In fact, one of the biggest names in comedy history, Robin Williams, came to Acme in 2008 to work on material for his return to stand-up, serving as a testament to the quality of crowds Minneapolis had become known for.

Outside of Acme, a new wave of comedy clubs and open mics began to pop up. A new club, Rick Bronson's House of Comedy, set up shop in the Mall of America, following in the footsteps of Knuckleheads from years earlier. Across the river, the Joke Joint Comedy Club offered a comedy alternative in St. Paul; Twitter comedy megastar Rob Delaney gave the club kudos in his autobiography for booking him regularly. Unlike in previous years, however, the clubs and performers worked far more collaboratively to create a comedy scene that nurtured performers and audiences, as opposed to competing with one another.

Another major development in Twin Cities comedy happened in 2000, when a scruffy music producer named Dan Schlissel decided to stop running a music label that mostly specialized in punk, metal, and alt-rock and instead turned his attention to producing comedy albums. He started Stand Up! Records, releasing hundreds of comedy albums from names like Lewis Black, Patton Oswalt, Maria Bamford, and Marc Maron. While the live aspect of stand-up comedy was beginning to simmer locally in Minneapolis once again, Schlissel was able to change the direction of comedy on the national level by growing Stand Up! Records into one of the country's most respected independent comedy record labels.

As for the earlier generation of performers, many, like Joe Minjares or Kristin Andersen, still perform sporadically, typically in smaller suburban venues in Maple Grove, Shakopee, and Mounds View. Others, like Fancy Ray, can still be found popping up on TV and at open mic nights, getting the star treatment from younger comics who are eager to soak up their knowledge and experience. Still others are happily retired from the stage and are more than comfortable letting the next generation of comedians carve their own paths.

While the names, stages, and styles have changed over the years, the spirit of Twin Cities comedy continues to burn just as brightly as it did all the way back in the late seventies. As long as there are stages with microphones and people who want to laugh, Minnesota will never stop being funny.

Acknowledgments

While this book came together with the help of dozens of comedians and club owners who played a role in creating and developing the incredible Twin Cities comedy scene, there are literally hundreds more who are responsible for helping it grow and thrive today.

A special thank-you to everyone who allowed me the opportunity to be a part of this incredible piece of comedy history and contributed to the making of this book: Scott Hansen, Louie Anderson, Jeff Gerbino, Alex Cole, Patrick Bauer, Jeff Cesario, Joel Madison, Scott Novotny, Priscilla Nelson, Steve Billings, Stephanie Hodge, Lizz Winstead, Dudley Riggs, Karen Pickering, Kristin Andersen-Anderson, Ken Bradley, Joe Minjares, Louis Lee, Peter Staloch, Josh Weinstein, John Bush, Matt Fugate, Tom Hansen, Rox Tarrant, Alex Jackson, Fancy Ray McCloney, Rick Carney, Paul Dillery, Colleen Kruse, Mike Brody, Mike Gandolfi, and Craig Allen.

Also, thank you to *City Pages, Twin Cities Reader,* and all the writers and journalists who helped put a spotlight on comedy locally before anyone else.

Finally, thank you to every comedian—from headliners to open mic-ers—in the Twin Cities past and present for having the desire to get onstage and make people laugh. Or at least try.

Selected Bibliography

Brauer, David. "No Laughing Matter." *Twin Cities Reader*, March 6, 1991, 8–11.

Gustafson, Amy Carlson. "Twin Cities Comedian 'Wild' Bill Bauer Dead at Age 62." *St. Paul Pioneer Press*, August 29, 2012.

Kaner, Elyse. "Comedian, Former Anokan and Mentor to Many, Remembered." *Anoka County Union Herald*, September 12, 2012.

Mabery, D. L. "St. Paul Medicine." *Skyway News*, October 10, 1990.

Protzman, Bob. "Funnymen Fight to Knock out Competition with Punchlines." *St. Paul Pioneer Press*, October 1, 1982.

Rybak, Deborah Caulfield. "Funny Bones." *Star Tribune*, July 11, 2004.

"Stand Up Comics." *Nighttimes*, KTCA, February 14, 1979.

Steele, Mike. "For Comedy, Come to the Cabaret, My Friend." *Minneapolis Tribune*, September 14, 1981.

Strickler, Jeff. "But Seriously Folks ... Amateur Comedians Take over Nightclub Stage, Get the Last Laugh on Skeptics." *Minneapolis Tribune*, October 6, 1978, 1–6C.

Winegar, Karin. "'Vomics?' At 2 Places, Novices Can Shtick It to Comedy." *Minneapolis Star*, March 16, 1979.

Index

About the Author

Patrick Strait moved to Minneapolis in 2007, and a year later he began writing for *City Pages,* where he was (at that time) the only writer regularly covering local comedy, including profiles about up-and-coming comedians, unique events, major club shows, and start-up open-mic nights. He has served as the regular comedy beat reporter for *City Pages, The Growler,* and Thrillist, writing more than fifty stories a year about all aspects of stand-up comedy in the Twin Cities. Beyond the major clubs  (Acme, House of Comedy, Joke Joint), he covers trends such as the growth of and breakthrough of Black and other comedians of color, an increased focus on diversity, and the cooperative nature of the local comedy scene that has helped it continue to grow and thrive. He lives in Minneapolis with his wife and two children.

The text of *Funny Thing About Minnesota . . .* has been set in Wolpe Pegasus, a typeface designed by Berthold Wolpe and remastered and digitalized by Toshi Omagari of the Monotype Studio.

Book design by Wendy Holdman.